LIFE!

Why We Exist...
And What We Must Do To Survive

MARTIN G. WALKER

First published by Dog Ear Publishing
4010 W. 86th Street, Ste H
Indianapolis, IN 46268
www.dogearpublishing.net

ISBN: 1-59858-243-7

This book is printed on acid-free paper.

Printed in the United States of America

Dedication

In memory of my father, Thomas Samuel Walker

Acknowledgements

My thanks to all of those who have provided moral and practical support in helping me write this book. In particular, thanks to my wife, Hope, and my children, Dorothy and Zane, for their patience with my absences while writing and for the inspiration of their love. Thanks to George and Billy for prompting me to think and to have faith in my thoughts. Thank you to Karen Brunson for her fine editing and unflagging optimism. And to Louis Begley, Chris Shields, and Mark Levy for reading advance copies of the manuscript and giving their invaluable thoughts and advice. Finally, a word of posthumous gratitude to Arthur Schopenhauer whose vast intelligence, insight, and wit first prompted the idea that formed the kernel of this book.

Author's Note

I hope you enjoy this book and that you find something valuable in its insights. As you will see, I have a lofty goal—to encourage us to look hard at why we're here, what it means to be alive, and to adjust our attitudes and behavior accordingly. Life can only evolve and survive if we acknowledge that the evolution and survival of life itself is more important than the evolution and survival of any one person or group.

I wrote this book with the hope and intention of communicating these ideas as broadly and effectively as possible. If you find meaning and value in this book, please tell a friend or acquaintance; pass the book on, or purchase a copy as a gift.

If you would like to comment on the book or purchase additional copies, please visit me on-line at: http://martingwalker.com OR http://www.myspace.com/martgwalker

Do not believe in anything simply because you have heard it. Do not believe in anything simply because it is spoken and rumored by many. Do not believe in anything because it is found written in your religious books. Do not believe in anything merely on the authority of your teachers and elders. Do not believe in traditions because they have been handed down for many generations. But after observation and analysis, when you find anything that agrees with reason and is conducive to the good and benefit of one and all, then accept it and live up to it.

-Siddhartha Gautama (The Buddha), 563-483 B.C.

Contents

Introduction

What an extraordinary thing a book is. You hold in your hands a bundle of papers glued together in a particular sequence. As you scan the words and sentences printed on the pages, your mind translates them into connected concepts. At the printing plant, a machine stamped ink onto the paper in the shapes of the letters that make up these words and sentences. The data describing the letters and their arrangement were stored for a while on a computer at the editor's office, and before that on my computer. And their virtual journey began many months before as I sat contemplating the impulse to communicate something, tapping out my thoughts through the pressure of my fingers on a keyboard.

The book you hold in your hands conveys a new set of concepts; it explains why we exist, what our lives mean, and how all forms of existence relate to one another. This new understanding takes its place in a line of inquiry that stretches back to Plato's ideas. It digs beneath the surface impressions of our lives and the world around us to show that a single fundamental principle accounts for the shapes and natures of particles, planets, and people alike. And it demonstrates how we can use the insight this principle provides to understand the lives we lead, our senses of morality, beauty, and spirituality, and our place in the continuum of existence.

* * * * *

Saturday is trash day in my neighborhood. It's also sidewalk sale day. Outside each house sits a small mound of plastic bags waiting for the garbage truck. And on various blocks, veteran vendors or hopeful neophytes haul out old rocking chairs and listless lamps and magazine racks with missing slats—things that might look like trash to some but that they intend to sell, and likely will, if not today then next week or the week after. At the end of one vendor's table, reaching up in a crooked steeple toward the blue aloofness of the April sky—each waiting to bring its author's concepts to a new mind—rest a few old books.

But as extraordinary as a book might be, are these any more extraordinary than their tablemates—the deco lamp with the broken shade, the ceramic salt and pepper shakers baked in yellow glaze? Is a book any more extraordinary than the small pebble that I absently kick out of my path as I push my son along in his stroller? That innocuous piece of rock which skitters off into the gutter was forged, millions of years ago, by the tremendous pressure of the cooling planetary crust, and this crust in turn was formed, millions of years before that, out of a spinning congealing mass of dust and gas. Every subatomic speck of material in that pebble came into being billions of years ago, a few moments after the universe began. Even the most mundane object, even the unwanted—the apparent detritus—of the world around us, the things we want to bury in a landfill and forget about: everything sings the miraculous song of existence.

Most of the time we don't hear this song. We have to get on with our lives, after all; we can't stop to marvel at the exalted journey of every pebble in our paths. But we do pause from time to time, shake our heads at the profound and purposeful mystery of the world around us, and wonder why we're here, whether existence has any meaning beyond the blind whirling dance of electrons in orbit about their nuclei. Why do we exist? Why does anything exist? For as long as people have asked questions we have asked ourselves and one another about the nature and meaning of our existence and the existence of everything we see around us. Some have stopped along the way, satisfied with the answer at hand—a divine hand, the big bang, nothing—but many have kept asking, not happy with an answer that rests on faith or begs the question.

Scientific analysis has provided us with an increasingly rich and thorough understanding of the substance and mechanics of the universe, explaining aspects of existence that once seemed obscure or mystical. We no longer believe that a pile of hay makes mice, or that the sun rotates around the earth. We know why the ocean tides wax and wane. We can see our insides by pulsing sound waves through our skin or firing X-rays through our flesh and up against our bones. The progress of scientific understanding over the past few centuries has been extraordinarily rapid. And yet, as scientists unwrap each new layer of understanding, they reveal another mystery beneath. Physicists hope to someday achieve a theoretical understanding of the material of the universe that will unify the explanation for the forces of gravity and electromagnetism with the nuclear forces that hold together the basic building blocks of matter—a theory of everything, thoroughly demystifying the mechanics of the physical universe. Biologists likewise strive for an ever more complete knowledge of genetic material and the complex physiological workings of living organisms, and they may one day unlock all of life's secrets.

But despite the shrinking sphere of the unknown, and even allowing for the possibility that we may one day achieve a complete and indivisible scientific explanation for physical and organic existence, those who seek philosophical or spiritual answers to the question of what it all means don't expect science to provide them. As science knocks down each door, philosophy and spiritual inquiry regroup behind the next, setting up their call anew. Science explains the what, but we still want to know why. Why does the universe exist at all, why do human beings exist, and why do we as individuals exist?

Although philosophy and spiritual inquiry agree that science can't provide the ultimate answers, they don't necessarily agree on what those answers may be, or even how to frame the questions. Philosophy rattles the tin can of skepticism, never happy with the easy and familiar, probing the limits of what we can truly know about existence through our experience of it. Conversely, theological or spiritual inquiry starts from the ground of faith and seeks to understand our place in the world through contemplation and inquiry of that ground; the spiritual answer is given, and we just need to let ourselves accept it.

As individuals, we tend to approach these questions more directly and urgently. We ask them when we encounter sadness or disillusion or when we witness hatred and abuse, enmity and struggle, misery and suffering. Every minute of every day someone somewhere in the world suffers, kills, starves to death—what meaning can explain this? Millions live in poverty, dying of starvation and disease, ravaged by war and natural disaster; millions have died through genocide. At the same time, the world teems with acts of love and caring, surprises us with beauty and peace, showers us with possibilities for happiness and enlightenment.

In each of our lives we encounter times of pain and despair, and moments of true happiness and contentment. In describing his experience of the Nazi concentration camps, Viktor Frankl (*Man's Search for Meaning*, 1946) talks about how he and the other prisoners, despite daily and unremitting torture, exhaustion, and deprivation, nevertheless felt excitement and happiness at the very small and very relative pleasures of camp life: a morsel of extra food, assignment to a particular work duty. (Frankl teaches that we find meaning in the substance of our lives, not outside that substance.)

As the days pass—some good, some bad—we try to make sense of this duality, to apply some consistent interpretation to how we think, feel, and act. Many of the explanations available to us invoke a force outside our immediate awareness and perception, some divine or nonphysical originator. And whether or not we have such faith, we typically approach life's concerns and questions by measuring our experience against our own political, moral, and social yardsticks, from whatever tree these may be whittled. We live by a set of beliefs, rules, and ideas that seem to make sense to us and by which we can judge our choices and the choices of others.

But often this approach leaves us unsatisfied with the completeness and rightness of our own choices, or fundamentally at odds with those who may live by a different set of beliefs, rules, and ideas. Many of us do not or cannot find in ourselves an unswerving faith in a particular ideology or sense of spirituality. We live uncertain of why we live and uncertain of what to do or how to behave in a particular situation, how to feel about ourselves and our choices, how to feel about others—often without hope and with no sense of higher meaning. Conversely, many of the world's chronic problems—war, oppression, terrorism—have their roots in ideological differences that arise when people have too much faith in their own convictions. Existential doubt and ideological intolerance are the twin plagues of consciousness.

As conscious beings, we inevitably strive for meaning. Consciousness first arises as an awareness of self in relation to nonself. As soon as we can frame the concept of a self, we are thrust toward the question of what this self represents, and how it differs from nonself. Without consciousness, there would be no basis for such questions; there would be no questions. And if the quest for meaning arises through consciousness, does this quest have relevance only as a function of consciousness; is it otherwise irrelevant and moot?

* * * * *

How do we know that we exist? How do we know that the world around us exists? We piece together our perception of existence from our direct impressions, from what we feel, see, hear, touch, taste, and smell. We could form a theory of these perceptions that ascribes no meaning or value to them: the world is a dream, an illusion. Although such a theory cannot be absolutely refuted, it can be rejected simply as unhelpful and unproductive. Instead, we accept that our sense of ourselves and the world around us corresponds to an existence that behaves in accordance with certain underlying principles.

Arthur Schopenhauer (*The World as Will and Representation*, 1818) proposed that although our immediate sensory experience gives us the representation of existence, we can never apprehend directly the underlying object of existence (which he calls the world's Will) that must lie outside space and time. But even though we can't directly perceive the underlying nature of existence, the material world does provide us with its representation. Whatever we can glean from the nature of the material world will be our sole and indisputable guide to the nature of the Will.

In other words, if we want to be satisfied with our existential answers, we must work from what we experience and understand, either directly or indirectly. We are free to ask what else is there, what is the meaning behind the objects of our experience, what caused all of this to come into being and why? But to be sure that our answers rest on truth and not conjecture, we must start and end with our experience.

* * * * *

Every child knows that if you want to annoy another child or frustrate a grown-up, you need only ask "Why?" in response to everything they say. Any answer to any question can be turned into a new opportunity to ask why. The child's mind revels in the excruciating torture and comedy of the seemingly infinite question. As adults, we encounter the same infinite frustration when we look for meaning. No matter what answer we come up with, it is always possible to ask for the meaning behind the meaning. Relief comes from the answer "Because it is so." When we have gone far enough, we have no reason to go further.

Some claim that we have already gone far enough. They assert either that we have no reason to look beyond our immediate experience for any greater or deeper meaning (atheism, pragmatism, realism, nihilism), or that faith provides meaning (we must accept the unknowability of a divine creator). In either case, they have answered, "Because it is so." Before we reach our own "because it is so," however, we should feel that we have exhausted the material of our understanding and our perception of reality.

It has been more than two thousand years since Plato first proposed that reality reflects a system of universal abstract concepts. He grappled with why—when we all seem to understand and agree that certain ideas such as good and bad, right and wrong, justice and injustice must have an absolute basis—we can't seem to define or agree on that basis. To this day, we find ourselves stuck on the same problem. We're forever rehashing Plato's dialogues. We still feel that there must be some fundamental basis for moral and aesthetic judgment, an objective definition of good and bad, but such a basis eludes us.

An objective why of existence must rest on our experience of the world around us. It must be clear and simple and must be something we can readily apply to any practical matter of existence. The answer, of course, is right here for us to find. Just as an old dog-eared book sits patiently on the yard sale table, slowly warming in the sun as the crowds drift by, so, too, the existential answer waits, sure and certain, and in plain view. We have all of the evidence of our senses to work from, as well as the wealth of understanding provided by our sense of being and our indirect knowledge of the workings of the physical universe. We make judgments of good and bad, right and wrong, every day. Instinctively, intuitively, indisputably, we all have access to the answer.

This book uncovers the answer to why we exist and shows how it rests on a fundamental, universal principle. Armed with this understanding it describes how we can articulate and explore those issues that otherwise seem dauntingly subjective and intractable, the concerns that divide us along lines of faith, geography, or politics. It guides us toward a new way to structure the dialogue about our differences, to expose the non-answers and the sophistry of ignorance, and to replace them with a sense of deep meaning, peace, and existential purpose. Most important, it conveys a fundamental lesson about universal empathy that each of us must learn in order to help ensure the survival of the human race.

A human being is part of the whole, called by us 'Universe'; a part limited in time and space. He experiences himself, his thoughts and feelings as something separated from the rest—a kind of optical delusion of his consciousness. This delusion is a kind of prison for us, restricting us to our personal desires and affection for a few persons nearest us. Our task must be to free ourselves from this prison by widening our circle of compassion to embrace all living creatures and the whole nature in its beauty. Nobody is able to achieve this completely but striving for such achievement is, in itself, a part of the liberation and a foundation for inner security.

-Albert Einstein

Section 1: Understanding the Forms of Existence

Part 1—Understanding Material Existence

Framing the Question

Two old men sit at a chess board, silent except for the slight wheeze of their breath, intent on the arrangement of the game. The afternoon sun falls across the table, gilding the dust motes that float serenely through the air above. Each day at two o'clock they pull out the board, set up the pieces, and play. Over the years, their fingers have softened the contours of the chess pieces; the board's surface is worn and scuffed.

A brief commotion of feet signals the appearance of the host's grandson. He comes barreling into the room, breathless with energy and wonder, rushing headlong across the room and stopping a few inches from the board. The old men look up and smile at the ferocious and featherlight will of the child. "Who's winning?" he asks, staring down at the chess pieces as if the answer lies in the tilt of a knight's sword or the set of a castle's battlements.

When we ask about the meaning of existence (when we want to know why we exist, why the universe exists as it does), we ask a very material, in-the-moment kind of question. But, as with the child and the chess game, we won't find our answer unless we look beneath the surface of things. That which manifests itself in the world around us came before space and time and therefore must exist outside space and time; we can't see it or touch it. (This concept appears in religious and spiritual doctrine, too—that is, whatever deity or creative force gave rise to the heavens and the earth can't be made of the same stuff as the heavens and the earth.) But everything that happens in the material universe must happen in accordance with the underlying why. Any answer must explain why we exist in this material form at this time—must explain the progress from nothingness to something and from the original something to the particular something that we perceive around us today.

Extension in space and progress in time begin and end with material existence. But the concepts of extension in space and progress in time, the rules of this existence, came before and live outside the material universe.

Take the architecture of a house. We won't find the architecture in the joists and beams, the bricks and mortar. The architecture existed before we built the house and will continue to exist even after the house has been destroyed. The architecture doesn't even exist in the form of a piece of paper on which we can see the architectural drawings—the drawings make a useful representation of the architecture, but burn them and, provided we have sufficient information, we can simply draw them anew.

Likewise, in a game of chess, the rules of the game guide the play and control the particular options available to the players, but they don't exist in the game; the rules don't appear in the pieces or the board. The players play in accordance with the rules, but the rules exist whether or not anyone plays the game. The rules don't even exist as words written on a piece of paper. Two versions of the rules will use different words to explain the same procedures. And even if we were to lose all of the written rules of chess, two players could still play the game.

Extension in space and progress in time work in accordance with the why of existence, but the why of existence doesn't require our space and time and can't be found in space and time. We will never commune directly with the why of material existence, but (as with the architecture of a house or the rules of a game of chess) the universe operates in accordance with certain rules, and we can begin to discern the why of existence through a keen observation of existence. Study a house; measure the angles and lengths, and you start to discern the architecture. Watch carefully as people play chess, and you begin to understand how the game works.

Our understanding of existence must be consistent with our experience, and our experience occurs in space and through time.

* * * * *

Our perception of space rests on the concepts of collocation and displacement. Two points in space either appear together (they are collocated) or apart (they are displaced). We experience space through our awareness of material objects, the things we touch and see. Our experience and our indirect observation tell us that space operates according to certain consistent underlying principles.

The principles of Cartesian geometry, for instance (parallel lines never intersect, and so on), which apply under nonrelativistic conditions, and Einstein's modified principles of space and time (the curvature of space, and the dilation of time), which apply under relativistic conditions, work consistently and according to expectation, regardless of where we are in the universe. And they work today as they did yesterday, and, as we can expect them to work tomorrow.

We experience space very directly through the physical sensation of our bodies. We take up space; we move through space. Our tactile and visual senses inform our awareness that we move through a consistent and essentially unbounded three-dimensional world. If we walk in a straight line from point A to point B today and then do the same tomorrow, the distance will remain the same.

We can reasonably assert the following: our experience of space is consistent and predictable because the principles shaping this interaction came before space and operate independent of space. Just as in a game of chess, the bishop moves diagonally because he is constrained to do so by the rules of the game.

Time operates according to the concepts of simultaneity and succession. We measure and experience time as a difference between two points of simultaneity. I wake up in the morning as the sun rises. My waking and the sun's rising occur simultaneously. Later, as I lie down to rest, I watch the sun set. I can measure the temporal distance between these two moments if I know how long it is between the sun's rising and setting.

Before the universe began, simultaneity and succession had no practical meaning—there was nothing to be simultaneous with anything else, nothing to succeed anything else. The passage of time as we know it originated in the moment of the big bang. Because nothing can travel faster than light, time (and space) proceeded outward from the big bang in all directions at the speed of light (strictly, the speed of propagation of electromagnetic radiation in a vacuum).

We experience simultaneity and succession through causality (events A and B cannot be distinguished by determining which one preceded the other—simultaneity; event D proceeds from event C—succession), and we interpret time by perception of the relative distance or difference between moments as compared to the distance between periodic events. We measure days by the coming and going of day and night, years by the coming and going of the seasons. We measure fractions of seconds by counting the oscillations of excited crystals.

Without these points of reference, without relying on the regular repetition of particular events at particular intervals, we cannot measure the passage of time through anything other than our sense of it, but we can still perceive simultaneity and succession through our perception of causality. If we drop a ball it falls toward the ground. We experience causality as the action of the gravitational force on the ball, which, when we let the ball go, causes it to accelerate toward the ground. The moment of letting go precedes the moment of reaching the ground. (Our experience tells us that time does not move in the other direction.)

All causes and effects contribute to this understanding, including the transfer of momentum from one moving object to another, the decay of radioactive isotopes, the aging of the cells in our bodies, the combustion of hydrocarbon-based substances such as wood, and the oxidization of some metals. Reinforcements of the perception of causality, the direction of time, appear all around us. Our perception of the world we live in, our understanding of the universe, rests fundamentally on the concept of time, of a causal succession in one direction.

We can assert that our perception is flawed, that the appearance that time moves in one direction is invalid, but this is inconsistent with our experience. Therefore such a theory, although interesting, does not help us understand the form of existence that we perceive. (Again, we seek a consistent explanation of why things appear to be as they are.) As with space, we can reasonably assert the following: our experience of time is consistent and predictable because the principles shaping this interaction came before time and operate independent of time. Returning to our chess analogy, the principle that the players take turns in making their moves operates as soon as the game begins and applies consistently to all games.

The rules of chess don't demand a game of chess, but as soon as a game of chess begins, the rules of the game will guide the play. So, too, as soon as the universe began, the rules of space and time shaped the process of its creation and expansion.

* * * * *

"Who's winning?" the child asks. He wants to know how the game is turning out; he is interested in the particular outcome. And in our search for an understanding of existence, we want to understand the particular, too. Why me, why us, why this planet?

The child has watched the old men play countless games of chess, but he wants to know about this game, today. Matter, as we know it, accounts for only a small percentage of the known energy in the universe, and electrons, protons, and neutrons are only three of the possible types of substantive particles—they have many siblings and cousins. We want to know why our world consists entirely of atoms that consist entirely of electrons, protons, and neutrons. We want to explain why these are the most common and abundant forms of visible existence. And we want to understand our own existence.

But why not shine the beam of our curiosity on that which gives rise to the strange and ephemeral—things that pop in and out of existence, never to be seen again? Shouldn't we be wary of a line of inquiry that focuses exclusively on explaining our form of existence and the world around us? Shouldn't the why of existence explain all of existence?

On the other hand, if we can't explain atomic and molecular structures, if we can't explain life, we won't have furthered our understanding of that which we are, in which we play an active role. If we know how every chess piece moves and operates but not that a player must trap her opponent's king in order to win, we can't play chess. We want to discern the overall design for material existence and to know where we fit in, how and why we came to exist as we do. (In answer to the child's question, the grandfather frowns slightly as his friend moves a rook forward. "Too early to say," he replies.)

The Illusion of Matter

I sit on a couch in my home, typing on my laptop keyboard; these words appear before me on the screen. It is winter. Night has fallen, and rain spatters against the window. The light from the electric bulbs in the chandelier overhead cast brightness and shadows around the room. Music from the stereo system plays in the background. Beneath me the house sits solidly on its foundations, as it has for over a hundred years. If I look to my left, I can see through the window the lights of the city in the near distance and a plane coming in to land at La Guardia airport. Through the pressure of my body on the couch and my fingers on the keyboard, I feel the weight of my physical being.

I understand that the earth, being massive, exerts a gravitational attraction on my body, giving it this sense of weight. I know that it gets dark at night because this portion of the earth's surface rotates away from the sun, as it does every day, and that winter reigns because the earth orbits the sun once every three hundred and sixty-five days, causing each hemisphere in turn to tip away from the fiercely burning star so that the warming rays arrive more obliquely. I know that our solar system forms part of a galaxy of stars, many with their own planetary systems, and that our galaxy in turn forms part of a galactic cluster. I know that all evidence points to a history in which these galactic clusters were borne from and flung out by an unleashing of tremendous amounts of energy in a cataclysm known as the big bang, and that for this reason the universe expands and may one day contract again (we're not yet sure).

I know that my nine-month-old son downstairs has genetic material that comes from my genetic material in combination with his mother's. I know that his mother and I both carry a genetic mutation that can result in cystic fibrosis, that this is a recessive mutation, and that there was thus a twenty-five percent chance that our son would suffer from cystic fibrosis (he does not, although he is a carrier, too). I know that the air between me and the loud-speakers behind me transmits the music I'm listening to by compression of the air molecules in longitudinal waves that my ear senses and transmits to my brain, permitting me to perceive these compressions as sound. I know that the objects I see around me—the electric lights and the computer screen—reflect or emit electromagnetic radiation in a range of frequencies that my eyes detect and translate into representations in my head. I understand that my body, the couch, the computer, and the rain outside (as well as every piece of metal, concrete, glass, and dirt in the city of New York) consist of molecules, and that these molecules consist of atoms. I know that the atoms consist of electrons, protons, and neutrons, which in turn consist of smaller particles that tend not to be household names, particles that scientists have coaxed into being by turning up the dials on their particle colliders.

These and similar observations and analyses of the material world we can accept or reject. For the most part, we accept the reality of our senses and the consistent explanations of scientific theory and experimentation to the extent that measurements and data support them. Most of us, most of the time, agree on the nature of the world around us.

* * * * *

According to our perception, the universe in general and the world we live in seem solid and predictable. Our feet press firmly against the ground. The earth turns its slow circle around the sun. We measure change in years, decades, centuries, and millennia.

Some changes happen more rapidly than we expect them to, causing us alarm. We worry about the resilience of the planet's ecosystem—global warming, ozone depletion, the extinction of species, the exhaustion of fossil fuel reserves—but even these changes unfold according to processes that we can generally track and understand. For the most part, matter remains matter, radiation remains radiation, life continues to propagate. We each continue to live, to experience a self-consistent and continuous perception of reality.

But if we pause and reflect on that perception, we realize that it leads us into something of an illusion, a distortion. Our perspective as living organisms acts as a filter and lens for our perception of the world.

A drinking glass sits next to me on the table. I can see through the glass, even though it holds the water I poured into it. Photons (light waves or light particles) pass though the glass, their journey only slightly perturbed. The glass holds its form and feels solid to the touch because, at room temperature, the glass molecules bond together quite strongly, and the glass molecules hold their form because the atoms in the molecules bond to each other through electromagnetic attraction. Within the atoms, the electrons and the nuclei remain bound together. But if we take a microscope and look at the glass, gradually increasing the magnifying power, we see that at each level of magnification, the apparent material substance of the glass melts away. The glass is a lot of empty space punctuated by the tiniest of particles held together by forces of attraction.

We perceive objects, such as the glass, as having solidity because the form of our own existence has a similar solidity. When I reach out and touch the glass, my own bodily structure (my skin and flesh) remains separate from the structure of the glass. The bonds that maintain the molecular and underlying atomic structure of my hand, and the bonds that maintain the structure of the glass, have sufficient strength to keep the two separate and distinct.

Our perception of matter presents a considerable challenge to our understanding of the underlying nature of existence. We consist of matter. Everything we interact with consists of matter. In our everyday experience, matter remains impermeable, durable, and solid. But as far back as 1911, Ernest Rutherford found that when he fired helium nuclei at a thin sheet of gold, almost all of them passed right through. Atoms aren't tiny solid spheres; they're mostly empty space. We perceive existence through our physical bodies, and this physicality prevents us from being immediately aware of the underlying form of matter.

Our other senses, too, tend to limit and constrain our perception. I hear the music from my stereo system because my ears are tuned to a particular slice of the audible spectrum. Air compressions exist at frequencies both below and above those we can hear. Our eyes register frequencies across a fairly narrow band in the electromagnetic spectrum. This tuning narrows our sense of the world around us, limits and distorts our perspective on existence. If we could hear frequencies below the current range of human hearing, we would be able to sense the approach of storms, as many animals can. If we could see X-rays, many objects that we now think of as opaque would appear translucent. Our form of being greatly influences the way we perceive the world around us.

* * * * *

Matter fills the world of our immediate perception. Everywhere we look we see matter; everything we do brings us into contact with matter. Matter seems solid and reliable, ever-present—it seems fundamental and irreducible. But to understand the why of matter, we need to get past the what, or more correctly, to get past our immediate sense of the what.

Over the last two hundred years, our understanding of the material world has proceeded quickly. Scientific analysis and the methods of scientific investigation have allowed us to see ever more deeply into the nature of physical existence. We can track the arc of life on Earth through the record of fossils and genetic research. We know roughly how living cells reproduce. We understand that DNA codifies the information that gives organisms the ability to pass on traits, or to mutate. We've analyzed how the matter of our bodies and the world around us results from different combinations of a few dozen naturally occurring elements (hydrogen, nitrogen, sulfur, carbon, and so on). We know that atoms result from combinations of three subatomic particles—protons, neutrons, and electrons, and that neutrons and protons in turn consist of quarks. We've established increasingly sophisticated models for gravity and electromagnetism.

We've found that, at the subatomic level, particles don't always behave like particles, that we can no longer think of them as tiny spheres spinning around each other, and that it is often more appropriate to describe them in terms of waves (oscillations) or probability states. (Aim a single electron at two tiny holes and, unlike a solid particle, which could only pass through one hole or the other, the electron passes through both of them at once, causing a wavelike interference pattern at the far side.) At the subatomic level, substance gives way to likelihood. Schroedinger's equation presents the startling conclusion that we can't pin down a sub-atomic particle—either we know where it is or we know how much energy it has, but we cannot precisely know both at the same time. Einstein's famous formula $E = mc^2$ asserts that a change in mass results in a proportional change in energy. After Einstein, we need make no fundamental distinction between matter and energy.

$$* \quad * \quad * \quad * \quad *$$

The farther we look out into space, the farther back in time we can see. Light that has traveled for millions of years to reach us shows the universe as it was millions of years ago. We know that the progress of the universe over time has been one of expansion and cooling. Our solar system and the planets around the sun began as a swirling, superhot cloud of gases. As this whirling cloud gradually cooled, the planets spun off into orbit, cooling further. Even today, when we stand under a pale, heatless winter sky, feet and hands aching from the cold, far below the earth's frozen crust its core churns with molten lava.

At the moment the universe began, it didn't resemble the vast, differentiated structure we know today. Electrons, protons, and neutrons did not immediately spring into existence, whole and complete in sufficient quantities to account for an entire universe of material substance. The universe began with the release of huge amounts of energy (the big bang). At the very beginning, there were no particles, there was no matter. But very quickly, fundamental particles did spring up in vast quantities. So what is a fundamental particle?

As Einstein's equivalence of matter and energy implies, a fundamental particle is a form of energy. It is a particular energy state that is constrained to a finite, inelastic extension in three dimensions (as opposed to electromagnetic radiation, for instance, which propagates through space indefinitely in one direction). (See Appendix for further thoughts on the substance and quantization of space and time.)

To understand the emergence of matter and how this brought space into being, we need to first imagine the nonexistence of matter—a complete lack of material substance, an empty stage. The empty stage aches with potential. The audience shuffles restlessly, but the play has yet to begin. Then something happens. The first character comes on stage. At once she creates the world in which the play will unfold. (No actor, nothing; actor, something.) By the time the curtains close, the cast may number dozens of characters; collectively, they will have spoken hundreds of lines and conveyed countless emotions, thoughts, and actions. But without and until the appearance of the first actor, the play is nothing. So, too, before the appearance of the first fundamental particle, there was no material existence. The principles of existence prefigured the dimensions of space, but space had yet to appear.

The material universe came into being with the appearance of the first fundamental particle, a few fleeting moments after the big bang. Of course, this process of formation of material energy states didn't just produce one fundamental particle. The tremendous energy of the big bang gave rise to trillions upon trillions of fundamental particles. The outpouring of material substance has produced all of the billions of stars and planets that comprise the universe we live in today.

And once these particle energy states sorted themselves out, after much spontaneous transformation and interaction, the most stable energy forms—which turned out to be the atomic combinations of electrons and protons with neutrons—predominated. The material energy states in the cooling, expanding universe tended toward clusters of atoms, which then combined into molecules, clumped into stars and planets.

The inexorable congealing of this soup leaves us today living in a universe that seems to be full (and to have always been full) of an indestructible, durable substance we call matter. But if we take a sidelong look at the solid, impermeable structures in the universe—the galaxies and stars, the solar systems and meteor clouds—we can catch a glimpse of ourselves and all of this material substance as nothing more than a vast collection of energy states, tightly balled and held in suspension by the interactions between them.

The couch on which I sit, the keyboard at which I type, the raindrops that spatter against the window pane, the airplane hanging from an invisible tether below the hulking gray clouds: all of this consists of oscillations, probabilities, interferences, transformable energy in a state of relative stability. The appearance of solidity, of substance and extension, is an illusion, then, but we perceive this solidity because we, too, have a material form.

Why This and Not Some Other Matter?

Our world abounds with variety. The supermarket shelves heave with a bewildering array of brands and flavors. The natural world teems with species and subspecies. The earth churns with a profusion of metals, ores, minerals, and liquids. Yet, notwithstanding this enormous richness, every ounce of matter in the universe consists of atoms with only three components—electrons, protons, and neutrons.

We can't say that we won't find other forms of matter. Recent observations have led scientists to conclude that all of the known material of the universe, all of the stars and solar systems and galaxies, can't adequately explain its apparent mass and account for only a fraction of its total energy. Various theories have been put forward to account for the unseen mass and missing energy—dark matter, dark energy. The specifics of these theories (and whether those recent observations hold true) don't concern us here. For the present discussion, what's important is that we cannot presume that matter as we know it accounts for the only form of existence. But we can assert that the form of existence we have taken, and the form of existence that predominates in the world we know and interact with (our world: our solar system and the rest of the *visible* universe, every rock and tree, every cereal box on the supermarket shelf), consists not of lambda or omega nuclei orbited by neutrinos, but of protons and neutrons orbited by electrons.

But we need to answer why this is so. It is not, as was once thought, that these are the only possible types of particles. Although they have cornered the market on atomic existence, electrons, protons, and neutrons come from quite large families of particles known as leptons and hadrons. And although leptons seem to be truly fundamental particles, hadrons result from combinations of still smaller particles known as quarks. The electron (which is a lepton) has six brothers and sisters—the muon, the tau, the neutrino, the muon neutrino, and the tau neutrino. (Each lepton also has an antimatter twin, known as an antilepton.) Quarks, which come in six types, don't exist as free particles but combine in pairs or triplets to form mesons and baryons, collectively known as hadrons. (The proton and the neutron each consist of three quarks.) There are dozens of hadrons.

We begin to understand why atoms are ubiquitous when we look at the properties of the members of these particle families: the electron and the proton are the lightest and therefore the most stable of the lepton and hadron families. The more massive leptons and quark combinations don't last very long before breaking up into lighter particles. Of the leptons and quark combinations that do remain stable, only electrons, protons, and neutrons group together into naturally stable structures. In an atom, electromagnetism keeps the negatively charged electrons tightly bound to the positively charged protons. Nuclear forces bind protons and neutrons in the atomic nucleus.

Although the neutrino (a lepton quite similar to an electron but with no electromagnetic charge) is also a stable particle, and although the universe produces neutrinos in great numbers, their lack of an electromagnetic charge means that neutrinos can't bind electromagnetically with protons as electrons do, and therefore they don't form atomlike structures. Instead, neutrons fly through space, unbound and disconnected from the physical structures of stars and planets.

The proton has an effectively infinite life span. It is the only hadron that doesn't spontaneously degenerate into another hadron plus radiation. By comparison, the neutron, when not bound, has an expected life span of less than eleven minutes. But when bound with a proton in an atom's nucleus, the neutron can last indefinitely. Therefore, despite the dozens of fundamental particles and the many ways in which they could (statistically) be combined with one another in atomlike structures, atoms consist entirely of electrons, protons, and neutrons because other particles either quickly decompose or can't combine into stable structures.

* * * * *

Why don't leptons and hadrons come in more shapes and sizes? What universal principle dictates that leptons and quarks are the only fundamental particles? And how do we explain that protons don't vary from one to the next—a proton is a proton is a proton?

After all, electromagnetic radiation, another abundant energy form, seems to exist across a continuous spectrum of frequencies (and wavelengths). It covers everything from visible, ultraviolet, and infrared light to microwaves, radio waves, X-rays, gamma rays, and all points in between. One might expect, since electromagnetic energy exists across a seemingly continuous spectrum, that material energy also covers a continuous spectrum. But as far as we can tell, this isn't the case. With only a few handfuls of fundamental particles, we're led to conclude that material energy can take on only a small number of discrete values. We don't see fat electrons and skinny electrons. After accounting for variations predicted by quantum and relativistic effects, we find that leptons and quarks have consistent masses and therefore consistent energies.

The universe is not infinitely divisible, any more than it is infinitely large. Time and space are finite; they are made up of very, very tiny (but finite) indivisible chunks (see appendix). These chunks are created and occupied by the fundamental particles that make up material existence. We don't know why these chunks aren't a little bigger or a little smaller. We don't even know that this question has a meaningful answer—that the answer isn't arbitrary, or effectively arbitrary. But we do know that there is a pattern and a consistency to the material world we live in. We know that fundamental particles appear in a fairly large but finite number of types and sizes, and we know how this variety comes to be narrowed so that the material universe we live in consists predominantly of electrons, protons, and neutrons in the form of atoms.

Understanding the meaning of and explanation for the organizing principles behind the material world of which we are a part doesn't mean that we ignore the possibility of other types of existence. We have no reason to doubt that a particular explanation for the why of material existence as we know it will be inconsistent with an explanation for the why of any other kind of material or even nonmaterial existence. We will see that the opposite holds true—that the principles of existence apply regardless of the nature of the underlying nature of that existence, matter or not, atom or not.

So What Is the Why?

When I bake a cake, I can follow someone else's recipe or concoct my own. If I follow a recipe, I take eggs and flour and butter and sugar in the proportions given and go step by step through the directions, turning on the oven so that it reaches the right temperature, separating the egg yolks from the egg whites, whisking the whites, folding in the sugar and butter and flour. I grease the baking tin, pour in the batter, put the whole thing in the oven, and make a note of the time. A half hour later, the kitchen fills with the smell of cake, rich and sweet and nutty. I take it out and test it with a cold knife. If the knife comes out clean, I know the cake is done; if there's batter on the knife, I quickly return the cake to the oven and wait a little longer.

If I start with a good recipe and follow the directions with sufficient rigor, and if I use fresh ingredients and have a well-calibrated oven thermostat, I have a decent chance of turning out an edible cake. (I will have less of a chance if I try to concoct my own recipe.) If we ask ten people to each bake a cake, chances are we won't end up with ten edible cakes. If we ask them each to make a black forest gateaux, we'll probably end up with fewer good cakes than if we ask for a simple yellow sponge with raspberry filling.

So it goes with the things that exist in the universe. We must have the right ingredients in the right proportions at the right temperature, and the recipe must be one that works. With an abundance of protons and electrons at very high temperatures, for instance, we have the perfect recipe for the creation of hydrogen atoms. The positive electromagnetic charge on the proton interacts with the negative charge on the electron, and voilà, we have a hydrogen atom.

But unlike a cake, which tends to disappear quickly if it turns out well, matter remains in existence until it spontaneously decays into some other form of matter (plus radiation), or until it combines with other matter as a part of a more massive conglomerate (two hydrogen atoms combining to form a helium atom, for instance).

* * * * *

With matter, two factors determine the tendency for something to exist—the chance of its coming into being, and the likelihood of its remaining in existence. If we know how likely it is for a certain kind of matter to come into existence, and how likely it is for this kind of matter to endure or to combine with other matter, we will know how common it is, how prevalent in the universe.

Science can explain the whats and hows of this particle or that particle, but from a philosophical perspective, everything we see around us exists because it is of a form that tends to come into being and to persist. Many energy states and fundamental particles came into being as the universe began, but only electrons, protons, and neutrons combined in structures that tended to persist.

Things that persist tend to exist in greater abundance than things that tend not to persist. Over time, as the universe expanded and cooled, the stable forms of material existence became relatively more abundant than the unstable forms; the forms that tended to persist predominated.

* * * * *

As we track the course of development of the material universe, we can observe at each step the influence of persistence. From the undifferentiated energy soup, the fundamental building blocks of matter emerged—leptons and hadrons milling around, decaying, spawning new states, interacting. The kinds of matter that can exist in a particular set of circumstances depend on the conditions. The reason that scientists use particle colliders to study odd particles is that it is only by creating very high energy collisions that these strange particles can come into existence. To look at it another way: at cooler temperatures or lower energies, new particle states or particle combinations become feasible, while others are no longer feasible.

At the very beginning of the universe, very high energy levels made it feasible for high energy particles to exist, and not feasible for combinations such as atoms to exist. But as the universe expanded and cooled, this circumstance began to shift. Massive, high energy particles couldn't be sustained, so they decomposed into lower energy particles. Because they don't spontaneously transform, even in low energy conditions, the electrons and protons naturally emerged in greater numbers than the rest. And as energy levels dropped even further, it eventually became feasible for electrons to combine with protons and neutrons to form atoms. (This process, known as big bang nucleosynthesis, began about a minute after the universe began and lasted only about three minutes, after which conditions were too cool to allow fusion.) Even today, hydrogen atoms account for over ninety percent of all atoms in the universe.

The material that most interests us, because we consist of it (in the form of carbon, oxygen, nitrogen, sulfur, iron, and so on) is rare from a universal perspective, even though it's everywhere we look here on Earth. In our sun (and in other stars), the tremendous gravitational pull of the cumulated material and the very high temperatures create conditions under which fusion can occur. Fusion of solar hydrogen produces helium, which then burns to produce oxygen and carbon. The processes of fusion and combustion in an active star can produce elements up to the mass of iron (one atom of which has twenty-six protons in its nucleus). Unlike stars, planets aren't hot enough to maintain fusion. As a planet forms, the formative processes yield a different distribution of elements, as well as the production of elements heavier than iron (silver, tin, lead, for instance) and molecules.

Plotting the relative abundance of various atomic elements in the solar system reveals some striking trends. Generally, the higher the atomic number (in other words, the heavier the element), the less common it will be. (Hydrogen and helium, the two lightest elements, together account for over ninety-nine percent of the material mass of the universe; hydrogen accounts for seventy-five percent and helium, the next simplest and most abundant form, accounts for most of the remaining twenty-five percent.) This follows the principle that the more likely it is for something to come into being, the greater the tendency for that thing to exist. The heavier elements are less common because the processes that create them are less common.

Atomic elements with an even number of protons tend to be relatively more abundant than elements with an odd number of protons (this causes a zigzag effect). Atoms with an even number of protons tend to be more stable—the protons in an even-numbered nucleus can pair up with their spins opposing. Atoms with an even number of protons will therefore tend to persist more successfully than atoms with an odd number of protons.

Some elements (such as lithium and beryllium) appear to be relatively less abundant than one might expect given the general trend, and others (for instance, iron, nickel, and lead) appear to be relatively more abundant. The processes of atomic formation in a star tend to destroy lithium and beryllium; iron has a particular stability, however. The strong nuclear force, which binds protons and neutrons in the atomic nucleus, works most effectively at short distances. The electrostatic repulsion of the nuclear protons works against this. As nuclei get heavier, the electrostatic force starts to overpower the nuclear force. Bismuth, with eighty-one protons, is the heaviest stable atomic element. In iron, the nuclear force operates optimally, resulting in iron's greater stability and abundance. Again, the principle of persistence applies—lithium and beryllium are less likely to exist because they tend not to persist, whereas iron is more likely to exist because it tends to persist.

If we look at our immediate environment and the relative abundance of elements in the earth's crust, we see a very different picture. Ninety-eight percent of the earth's crust consists of just eight elements: oxygen (46.6%), silicon (27.7%), aluminum

(8.1%), iron (5%), calcium (3.6%), magnesium (2.8%), sodium (2.6%), and potassium (2.1%). This doesn't mean that the underlying principles have changed, however. The particular composition of the earth's crust results from the chemical processes that have formed the earth's outer layer. These processes favor the combination of these eight elements into molecules.

The situation changes again on the earth's surface. The graph in Figure 1 demonstrates the differences in composition of the earth's crust, the ocean, and plant life.

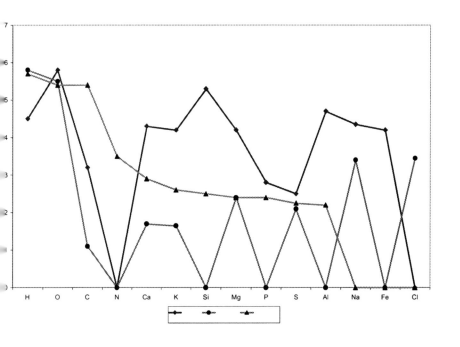

Figure 1. Relative abundance of the elements in the earth's crust, ocean, and plants. Data from Deevey, 1970, pp. 1–2.)

The particular processes at work in the formation of material substance vary dramatically, from big bang nucleosynthesis to solar fusion, planetary accretion, chemical reaction and combination, and the growth of living organisms. Despite these very different processes and the different proportions of substance they produce, the same principles apply: in any given system, if something is more likely to come into being, it is more likely to exist, and if something is more likely to persist (to remain in existence), it is more likely to exist. In the formation of elements through fusion and combination, these principles lead to the universal abundance of lighter elements (hydrogen and helium), tapering off dramatically as the elements get heavier (with a natural tendency to favor atoms with even numbers of protons). In the formation of the earth's crust and living material, the workings of chemical and organic combination become more important. But always the same principle of persistence holds true.

* * * * *

On a clear night, hundreds and thousands of stars are visible to the naked eye. We know that in addition to the stars we see, countless more exist—billions of them. Often, these stars come with systems of orbiting planets, much like our own solar system, and often such planets have moons.

After the end of the period of big bang nucleosynthesis (four minutes or so into the existence of the universe), clouds of superhot material swirled in all directions. Over time, the universal glop began to separate into independently rotating clouds, each with its whirlpool of superenergetic, superhot material. This material gradually formed the galactic and stellar structures we see today.

But why these structures? Why galaxies and stars and planets?

The child who learns to ride a bike soon discovers that happy medium between the wobbliness of going too slowly and the wipeout panic of going too quickly. Bikes work because the outward momentum of spinning wheel works against the inward tension of wheel spokes to create a system with greater radial stability than that of a nonspinning wheel. The same principle applies to a coin rolled across a table: at first it proceeds straight and tall, then it starts swaying and turning as its momentum subsides.

So, too, with the swirling clouds of material in the exploding universe. A cloud of particles spins outward, driven by the propulsive force of the big bang, but then it clamors together into a denser cloud, pulled by the force of gravitational attraction. The outward thrust of the spin and the inward pull of gravity eventually reach a balance: the cloud becomes a sphere, and the sphere becomes a star. A similar process occurs with the collection of stars in galaxies.

Planets form through the wipeout syndrome. A spinning cloud of material has too much outward momentum, and a portion of it breaks away from the main body, spinning off to form a smaller sphere, but staying in orbit around the bigger body, again held in balance by gravity.

This balancing process between opposing forces produces macroscopic structures that tend to persist over time. The universe constantly throws up new surprises for us to ponder and explain— stars that exist in pairs, stars that are dying, black holes…but these objects seem remarkable only because the rest of the material universe exhibits such consistency. Stars and planets account for the vast bulk of material substance in the universe because these structures formed naturally from the outward propulsion of vast quantities of formative glop, and because they tend to persist.

* * * * *

The various processes of thermonuclear fusion, combustion, gravitational and electromagnetic attraction, and chemical combination led to the formation of all of the material structures in the universe. These processes give rise to the relative abundances of atomic matter that we see around us according two very simple parameters—the chance that the process will happen, producing a particular form of material, and the chance that this material will remain in existence.

From a philosophical perspective, the same two principles and only these two principles govern the why of all material existence. Causality says: that which will happen will happen, and that which won't happen, won't happen. Our observations of the process of universal creation tell us: that which is more likely to happen will tend to happen more often than that which is less likely. And that which is likely to remain in existence will tend to remain in existence.

These principles work through different processes depending

on the particular conditions, but they apply always and under all circumstances regardless of location or time. The principles, then, are independent of space and time (as they should be) and don't require any form of material existence in order to be valid. We could characterize the why of existence as opportunistic—it seizes on that which is likely to exist and likely to persist.

Using only our observations of the processes that led to the formation of the universe and the planet we live on, we have derived a fundamental understanding of the why of material existence. The formative processes may be complex and sophisticated and will vary dramatically from one set of circumstances to another, but they always operate in accordance with the principle of persistence.

Abundance Isn't Everything

I have briefly discussed variety already, but in a world where (seemingly) every street brews up a Starbucks and the same song plays on the radio every half hour, sameness and ubiquity seem to be increasingly common and, at times, unwelcome. And although in looking at the why of material existence, we've focused on the opportunistic tendency for the processes of universal creation to favor the likely and the stable, we should remember that the existence of a multinational conglomerate doesn't eliminate the possibility that a corner store will pop up or remain in business—the overriding odds against its success don't eliminate its right to exist.

What I mean is that unlikely or nonpersistent forms don't have a lesser claim to existence than persistent forms. Relatively unstable or short-lived forms of existence play a critical role in existence or the process of creation. (Every aspect of material existence resulted from the transformation of energy from another form—we would have no material existence if not for the transformation of unstable energy forms.) The mechanisms of formation, of coming into existence, are blind to the ultimate persistence or nonpersistence of the resulting form. Or, to put it another way, the process of origination does not discriminate according to the result.

To truly understand and accept the nature of existence, we need to embrace the transient and ill-fated, the ephemeral and unstable, the nonpersistent. We will see how this understanding has a profound effect on our perception and interaction with the world around us. We must also acknowledge, however, that existence will be dominated by and will tend toward the likely forms and those that persist.

Entropy—The Achilles Heel of Material Existence

As Friday rolls around, it brings the relief of a workweek winding to a close, the expectation of a restful, fun, and productive weekend. Friday night is wonderful; Saturday morning is great, Saturday afternoon and evening just dandy. But on Sunday, things start to seem a little less breezy and carefree. By Sunday afternoon, the relative drudge and cares of the workweek loom again; I feel all too keenly that the weekend will inevitably come to an end, and Friday afternoon seems a distant memory and a long way off.

But does this mean that I should stave off my excitement and pleasure at the end of the workweek? Should I reduce my enjoyment in order to reduce my disappointment that it won't last forever?

According to the second law of thermodynamics, the entropy (the measure of disorder) of a closed system will tend to increase. Since the universe is a closed system, this means that the overall energy of the universe tends toward uniformity. Stars dissipate light and heat. Planets slowly lose momentum. Material objects absorb radiation. In all cases, energy states tend to equalize. Entropy reflects a pessimistic process—the universe is headed toward undifferentiated coldness. The development of new forms of existence will not go on indefinitely but will eventually go into decline—the stars will go cold, the conditions for the origination and sustenance of life as we know it will not last.

In metaphysical terms, although material existence spawns structures and processes of astounding sophistication and beauty—all in accordance with two very simple principles (that which is more likely to happen will tend to happen more often, and that which is more likely to persist will tend to persist)—the material manifestation of the universe has no goal or purpose, not even to go

on getting more fabulous. Material existence has no purpose. But
before you close the book in disgust, I should point out that it does
not follow, as we shall see, that within this ultimate purposeless-
ness we can find no meaning.

Section 1: Understanding the Forms of Existence

Part 2—Understanding Life

Life: The Significance of Form

New Yorkers who live in the borough of Manhattan don't much like to venture out to Brooklyn, or to schlep to Queens or the Bronx or Staten Island. When I lived in Manhattan, I felt the same way. The outer boroughs seemed such a long way off, so hard to get to, their geography and customs so impenetrable. To a Manhattan dweller, New York City is bounded by the Hudson and the East rivers and is just about as big and self-contained as it needs to be. Everything has a place and purpose: the office towers downtown; the maze and muddle of the villages, East and West; the bland bureaucracy of midtown; the snoot of uptown; the shabby excitement of the far-flung fringes; the blinkered, compromised oasis of Central Park. Why go any farther east than the South Street Seaport, any farther north than Harlem?

But of course some of us do. Driven out by high rents, lured by the relative peace and quiet, or just plain curious, we cross a bridge or skulk through a tunnel and find a whole new perspective waiting for us. Nowadays, I can't bring myself to want to go into the city to eat or go out at night. It just seems so unnecessary. I have most everything I want right here in Brooklyn. When I'm in the city during the week to work, the traffic and busyness feels labored and functional. The tourists wander about with their looks of glazed wonder, not knowing what they're missing.

So, too, once the course of universal existence got into its stride, it plodded on for billions of years, churning out stars and galaxies and planetary systems, flinging in the odd meteorite cloud for good measure. Everything was inanimate matter. The principle of persistence worked through the forms and structures and forces of fundamental particles, atoms and molecules, galaxies and solar systems. And then, a few billion years ago, the course of existence crossed a bridge. That which had been constrained by the forms and possibilities of inanimate matter suddenly found a new form, a new set of possibilities: life.

Life, or animate existence, interests us in particular because it is the form of our own existence. As a form of existence it differs dramatically from inanimate existence. With inanimate existence, a type or category of matter remains fixed and immutable. Once we determine that carbon has six protons in its nucleus, we know that carbon has always had and will always have six protons in its nucleus. If we exert sufficient force to add another proton to a carbon nucleus, we haven't changed the form of carbon—we've created a new instance of the form of nitrogen. The living form, by contrast, is constantly changing. No two instances are identical. Frogs, human beings, ferns—every type of living organism comes in all shapes and sizes. We identify the different types by their essential characteristics, but we know not to expect these to remain the same over time.

And yet, despite life's abrupt departure from the form of inanimate existence, with its appearance no new rules of matter or principles of existence sprang forth. Living organisms consist of the same stuff as earth and rocks and water, nothing more than atoms and molecules. And the same principles of existence apply to the living form, as they must to all forms of existence, regardless of time, type, or location.

With inanimate matter, the material itself absorbs our full interest—its composition and durability, its relative abundance, the forces and processes that brought it about and hold it together. But with animate matter—with life—the material itself interests us only insofar as it contributes to the form of the living thing. Inanimate matter works blindly and with no initiative; it moves and changes according to physical and chemical laws. Place a rock on a table and it will stay put, will remain just as it is—granite or limestone, marble or pumice—unless and until it is acted on by some external force. But with the appearance of the first living organism, and in any organic living process, the material form is subordinate to the existence and transformation of another form—the form of life.

Although the form of life operates by the same principles of existence as inanimate matter, it has an existence independent of the form of matter. Life as a form requires material existence, living organisms have physical bodies, and the matter that makes up a living organism is still subject to the why of existence, but the form of life permits this why to reveal itself in a new way.

We can imagine a cartoon artist with his flip-book. On each page he draws the same character, each image varying slightly from the image on the previous page. He carries the essential form of his character from one page to the next, creating a story that can only be discerned when he flips the pages rapidly. The character isn't embodied by any one of the drawings but comes to life through the succession of one drawing from the next. So it is with the form of life. Each new iteration, each generation, each species represents another page in the story of the form. We can't understand life by looking only at the individual organism or species. The form of life reveals itself in the flow from one instance to the next, and without this flow it is nothing. There can be no form of life unless living organisms continue to propagate. Life as a form of existence embodies a new imperative—it must further its own persistence.

And so we have identified the essential characteristic of life as a form: self-propagation. Each individual living organism survives for a short time, but just long enough to pass on its essential characteristics to the next generation, to further the existence of life as a form. Life as a form continues to exist because it passes on its form from one instance to the next.

All species, however different from one another, represent life as a form. When we look at the richness of variation in the form of life on earth—the bewildering varieties of plant life, from seething jungles to towering redwoods hundreds of years old—when we see how each animal strives to exist, to eat and grow, to mate and raise its offspring, we can easily forget that all living things exist not only in and of themselves but as part of the form of life. The thing being propagated, the thing that persists, is the living pattern, the form of life. Living things themselves do not persist indefinitely. Living forever provides no advantage to the form. Living things grow and propagate their variations of the life form through reproduction; they live to live, but they exist to create copies of themselves, to perpetuate the form of life.

What Is Life?

Before we are conceived, the various bits of matter that we will metabolize throughout our lives, that will become part of our physical being, are scattered around the world. If I could trace the journey of the bowl of cereal I eat today at breakfast, for instance, I might find that some of the nutrients in the oat flakes have been absorbed from the soil of an Idaho grain field. When we die, our families burn or bury the material of our physical bodies, which go back to being bits of inanimate matter. In between, we exist as particular instances of the human form.

To paraphrase the existential detective played by Dustin Hoffman in the movie *I Heart Huckabees*: every atom in our bodies has been forged in the furnace of the sun; isn't that cool? To take this one step further, every proton, neutron, and electron in every atom of our bodies emerged from the superhot energy soup just a few moments after the universe began. Everything that has happened since—all of the separation and differentiation through time and space—doesn't alter the underlying sameness of everything.

Looked at pragmatically, each living organism consists of a complex interrelated collection of molecular structures. The molecular structures grow and sustain the living organism by metabolizing nutrients from the outside world (through photosynthesis and absorption, for plants, and by feeding and respiration, for animals). In all of this, the molecular structures operate according to a particular pattern or model, and they carry this pattern's operating instructions encoded in their molecular structure. A key feature of the pattern is the ability for the living organism to communicate an approximate copy of itself from one iteration (one generation) to the next through reproduction.

Opinions vary on how life came into being, and on whether we should think of life's appearance as something relatively likely or extremely unlikely in universal terms. How many planets may there be on which some variety of the form of life exists, did exist, or could exist? How many of them may be similar to our planet, with varieties of life that we would recognize?

We could postulate that life appeared on earth through the confluence of highly unusual and unlikely circumstances. Or we could postulate that, given a fairly broad range of conditions on a cooling planet, the appearance of life was highly likely. But either way, life does exist; we live. In reaching for the why of our existence, it makes no practical difference whether living organisms struggle for an answer to the same question on millions of other planets, or on none. We want to know why we exist at all, what led to our particular existence, and whether we can put this into a context that will explain its meaning. We can only understand the why of our existence through achieving an understanding of life as a form, no matter how likely or unlikely this form might be.

Three essential qualities distinguish life as a form—reproduction, a self-sustaining metabolism, and mutation. Without reproduction, life as a form would have stopped at the single-celled amoeba. Reproduction represents the flipping of the pages, the transfer of the possibility of continued existence from one generation to the next. Living organisms reproduce in myriad different ways—seed dispersal, pollination, egg fertilization—but all living things must reproduce somehow or face certain extinction.

And in order to survive long enough to reproduce, we need to eat and grow. Again, plants and animals have developed many different systems by which to take in nutrients and absorb energy, but each successful plant and animal must take in enough food from its environment to be able to live to maturity.

Finally, mutation is an essential quality of the living form, because it permits adaptation and diversification. Genetic material carries the patterns and rules by which each living entity operates, including instructions for the transmission of approximate copies of these patterns or rules from one iteration of the entity to the next. Variation in the genetic instructions, or mutation, is built into the reproductive cycle. Mutation is not a mistake; it is a marvelous mechanism for permitting changes in the organism's structure. Adaptation results from a successful mutation. A particular mutation may equip the new organism with a life pattern that leads to relatively greater success, or success in a different way, or protection against a change in external circumstances.

The mutative quality of life leads to a broad variety of organisms, each of which can be successful in its own way, as well as to a particular focusing or narrowing of particular types or traits that prove successful. The earth hosts huge numbers of species and subspecies. Many similar or closely related plants and animals thrive side by side. The variation between them doesn't necessarily lead to an either-or situation in which only one particular variation can succeed. If we study an extinct species, we typically see that extinction came about because the particular variation of the form of life couldn't compete or adapt. (Dinosaurs largely disappeared from the earth after some abrupt environmental change. But many animals still thriving today—such as alligators and elephants—trace their ancestry back to and differ very little from animals that lived side by side with the dinosaurs.) Mutation then serves two functions: it gives species the capacity to adapt to certain adverse changes in their environment. And it increases the number of variations of the form that exist, increasing the chances that some of those species will continue to exist.

Persistence in the Form of Life

It is springtime as I sit down to write. This morning I ran under canopies of green and white and pink, leaves and blossoms vibrant on the rain-blackened branches, beside yards churning with yellow hyacinths and daffodils. Life reaching up and out. And in the houses and apartment buildings flanking the streets, thousands slumbered, brewed coffee, made love, read the newspaper…Our particular perception of the world presents us with a perspective in which life, the urgency and necessity of life, seems undeniable and irrepressible.

With inanimate matter, the why of existence revealed itself through the principles of coming into being and persistence. Inanimate forms that tend to come into being will tend to exist. Inanimate forms that tend to persist will tend to exist in greater abundance than those that don't persist.

With the form of life, no new principles of existence came into being, and so these two same principles still apply, but they apply to the form of life rather than to a particular individual or thing. To illustrate this difference, we can compare the hydrogen atom with the fruit fly. The hydrogen atom persists as a form because hydrogen atoms tend to persist—many hydrogen atoms that came into existence billions of years ago still exist today. But the variety of the form of life that we know as the fruit fly persists because the fruit fly archetype persists. (Individual fruit flies live only a few days, just enough time to spawn the next generation— the next incarnation of the fruit fly type.)

The fruit fly's life span is shorter than the half-life of some unstable atomic isotopes. If we start with a thousand atoms of gold-198, which has a half-life of about three days, after three days we'll have only about five hundred remaining gold-198 atoms. After another three days, that number will have dropped to about two hundred and fifty. If we start with a thousand fruit flies, however, most of them will have died within three days, and certainly after five or six days we wouldn't expect any of the original fruit flies to remain alive. (Individual fruit flies don't persist.) But, presuming that our fruit flies have had some access to nutrients and to one another, the total number of fruit flies may not have dropped at all. We may even have many more than one thousand fruit flies. It is through the fruit fly type that the principle of persistence appears and operates. The fruit fly archetype persists even though each fruit fly has a relatively short life span.

To better understand persistence in the form of life, we can go back to the three essential characteristics of the living form— reproduction, self sustaining metabolism, and mutation. The most primitive varieties of the form of life, single-celled organisms, appeared through chemical and physical processes rather than by reproduction. But to persist, the form of life must generate new instances of itself. It must reproduce. To ensure persistence of a particular species, each generation, on average, needs to produce sufficient offspring to guarantee a growing population. Individuals in some species (frogs, for instance) produce hundreds of offspring, most of which won't reach maturity. In other species, our own included, individuals produce relatively few offspring, but each has a much greater chance of reaching maturity.

Each living organism must take in and metabolize the nutrients it needs to grow and sustain itself. And the physical structure of the organism must provide it with sufficient protection from harmful conditions and predators. Some plants and animals can go for long stretches without sustenance and can survive in the harshest conditions. Other organisms have far less resilience—the hummingbird, for instance, which must feed almost constantly in order to survive. Either way, a particular type of organism can only persist if the instances of that type live long enough to reproduce successfully. (In animals, successful reproduction also implies that each generation gets the care and protection it needs to grow to maturity.) Fruit flies reproduce relatively quickly and therefore needn't live long to ensure the perpetuation of the fruit fly type. Human beings reproduce more slowly, and therefore we must live substantially longer than fruit flies to ensure the success of the human species.

Mutation contributes to persistence by enabling variation and adaptation. By changing slightly from one generation to the next, each type of organism and the form of life in general improve their chances of persistence. Some mutations work against persistence, but without mutation there can be no successful adaptation. If the fruit fly didn't constantly and quickly mutate, the species would be vulnerable to changes in its environment; it would be defenseless against new threats. The rate and range of possible mutation in a particular species needs to be appropriate to that species. (There will always be the possibility that a disruption occurs too quickly for the species to respond to through adaptive mutation, leading to extinction, but for the form of life to persist, the adaptive effects of mutation must tend to outweigh this possibility.)

It is not clear whether, in some cases, external circumstances might not positively influence the way in which a species mutates. A species in which the material of the species' DNA changed, not from one generation to the next, but within a generation, could transmit beneficial traits more successfully than disadvantageous traits. (Genetic engineering, through conscious intervention, makes this, in practical terms, more a reality than a hypothesis.) Such a species would be more tenacious and successful, without changing the fundamental principles by which life operates.

All essential aspects, and many nonessential aspects, of the form of life contribute to its continued persistence. Having come into existence, the purpose of life is to remain in existence.

The Three (or Four) Aspects of Persistence of Living Things

This morning it rained. The light rainfall was just enough to make the roads wet and treacherous. In a while, I'll go out with my family, maybe see a movie. When I cross the street, I will try to be more careful than usual, to look out for cars that might not be able to stop as quickly on the slick pavement. I'll watch out for my family's safety: I'll take my twelve-year-old's hand, look out for my wife as she steps off the curb. And if we were to take one of our dogs along, I would look out for its well-being, too: I'd take a tighter hold on its leash if it were straining forward toward the street.

Without persistence, things cease to exist. As living organisms, we embody traits and characteristics that help us persist as individuals, as members of our species, and as instances of the form of life. Our tendency to persist is revealed in our growth and development, our ability to respond to threats, our instincts to sustain and protect ourselves and our families, and our needs and desires to endure and learn and reproduce. The tendency to persist comes before and works through all of our characteristics. Life as a form strives to persist; its continued persistence is imperative.

Each living organism persists by virtue of its capacity to sustain itself to maturity, to grow and feed and protect itself from harm. Species or types of living organisms persist through reproduction, the transmission of defining characteristics from one generation to the next. And the form of life persists through mutation, a gradual and inexorable modification of the type or species in such a way that new possibilities for its persistence appear (variation and adaptation). At any time, each aspect of an organism either contributes to the tendency to persist or is superfluous to it. The superfluous aspects will tend not to be propagated indefinitely (which is why we no longer have tails or webbed feet).

A particular living organism then contributes to the persistence of life as a form of existence at three levels—as an individual (by growing, sustaining, and protecting itself), as an instance of a type or species (by reproducing, and by nurturing and defending its own kind), and as a representation of the form of life (by carrying and transmitting the capacity for mutation, or by directly contributing to the success of other kinds of life). These are the three aspects of persistence of the living form. They do not work independently of one another—the form of life requires the species and the individual—but the aspects can conflict with one another, and through understanding this collaboration and conflict we can gain considerable insight into life as a form of existence, and our own lives in particular. We can also say that, because life requires material existence, a fourth aspect of the persistence of the living form is the persistence of matter itself.

When I look out for myself while crossing the street on a rainy day, I am exemplifying the individual tendency to persist, as demonstrated by my own urge to survive. When I turn and take my daughter's hand and look out for my wife as she steps off the curb (or even when I choose to have a family at all), I am exemplifying the tendency for persistence in the group or species. And if I take my dog with me and pull it out of the path of a speeding truck, I am exemplifying the tendency for life as a form to persist.

We can conceive of the importance of the persistence of material existence—the fourth aspect of persistence—if we think about how we might feel about the destruction of a mountain range. Without material existence, which gave rise to the universe, we would be nothing, and the entire seething tumult of universal existence would be nothing. A realization that reveals each fundamental component and facet of the universe as wondrous and essential.

*   *   *   *   *

What we mean by the persistence of the individual is unambiguous. My persistence is binary—either I exist or I don't exist; I am either alive or not alive. The persistence of each living organism covers its life span. That which contributes to a longer life span contributes to the individual's persistence. That which cuts short or reduces its life span reduces its persistence.

Similarly, life as a form either persists or doesn't persist. Before the first living organism came into existence, the form of life didn't exist. When the last living organism dies, the persistence of the form of life will have come to an end. Anything that tends to extend this span contributes to the persistence of the form of life.

But defining what we mean by the persistence of the particular type or species gets tricky. There are so many variations within a type, and types constantly change and evolve. Mutation is an essential characteristic of the form of life. Reproduction transmits only an approximate copy rather than an exact copy of the living form from one generation to the next. (We could argue, unhelpfully, that at the most fundamental level, each individual represents a type, and that no two individuals belong to exactly the same type.) As a practical and pragmatic matter, the tendency of the species to persist appears and has relevance over a wide spectrum—the type can be very broad (our desire to further the persistence of humanity), very narrow (the desire to protect our immediate families), or anywhere in between. It is not important that we establish a precise and exclusive definition of what we mean by *type*, but it is important to recognize that, in a particular situation, the broader the type, the bigger the contribution to the persistence of life as a form.

To understand our existence and our place in the world, we need to be able to clearly see how the different aspects of persistence affect the way we feel, react, and behave. These explorations will form the basis for understanding life as a willful, moral, and ethical phenomenon. In animals, for example, the tendency to persist underpins the urge for a creature to defend itself (the tendency in the individual), to defend its offspring (the tendency in the species), and—in some species—to defend other kinds of life (the tendency in the form of life itself). Hunger, anger, fear, desire, loathing, love, compassion, pain—every urge and impulse, every feeling and instinct, derives from the embodiment of the tendency to persist.

Objectively, although the form of life can't persist without individuals, the persistence of a particular individual has little or no effect on the persistence of life as a form. If I were to die tomorrow, the human species would continue to persist—people die every day; life as a form wouldn't even blink. Entire species become extinct without threatening the persistence of life as a form.

Subjectively, of course, each of us tends to experience the importance of our continued existence quite keenly. We have the urge to eat when we're hungry, to drink when we're thirsty. Unless we've lost the desire to live, we tend to take our self-protection very seriously, avoiding unnecessary danger and making sure to do what we can to live to a ripe old age. In the face of a threat, our tendency to persist appears as an instinctive, immediate, and reflexive urge to avoid or overcome the danger at hand. The tendency to look out for our own persistence is integral to our being; the resulting impulses are immediate and direct. We also experience what seems to be a direct urge to protect others, in particular those we know and love.

We embody the tendency for the persistence of the species through our ability to reproduce, which we experience directly as the sexual impulse. Humans respond indirectly to this tendency (as do many other animal species) through our sense of responsibility for the rearing and nurturing of our families, and through our sense of community.

The third aspect of persistence in the living form, the persistence of the form of life itself, works directly through mutation and indirectly through collaboration between different forms of life. Romantic and sexual attraction, for all its mystery, represents an indirect manifestation of the tendency to ensure positive mutation. Practically speaking, we tend to be attracted to people we like, people we want to have sex with, people we might want to raise a family with. Our attraction to some persons but not others has been cultivated over generations and baked into our genetic makeup. It tends to guide us toward mates with whom we will produce successful offspring. If attraction worked on a completely random basis or not at all, the form of life would suffer.

Less directly, when species live symbiotically (support one another) or do not willfully destroy one another, the form of life persists more successfully. Some species live in harmony, each contributing to the persistence of the other. As human beings, we have the capacity and very often the urge and instinct to intervene to protect other species.

We experience the tendency to persist, then, most strongly and directly as it applies to our own persistence, and less strongly and directly as it applies to the species and the form of life. Yet life as a form can only persist if the individual and the species are dispensable (individuals must reproduce and die in order for species to evolve; and, in evolving, a species must die, too). Yet again, though it may seem paradoxical, the persistence of the form of life also requires the persistence of the individual and the species. In other words, unless each living creature urgently pursues its own survival, the form of life won't survive.

The tension between the persistence of a particular species or type of life and the persistence of life as a form seems to have worked its way into our instinctive perception of the world. We simultaneously lean toward and recoil from the urgency and ruthlessness of mutation as a characteristic of life. We applaud and foster positive adaptation, the shedding of the unnecessary, the accretion of the useful or more accomplished—up to a point. At the same time, we pity or empathize with failure or nonadaptation, the wrong turn, the lame duck—up to a point. At our most noble and enlightened, we recognize change as an essential part of life's nature. But we fear change that seems too dramatic or threatens our way of life, because it conflicts with our urge to ensure the persistence of our own type. We can feel revulsion toward a regressive or unsuccessful change—again, because it seems to threaten the persistence of our species.

* * * * *

All living things embody the urge for self-preservation. Plants suck nutrients from the soil and bend toward sunlight. We jump out of the way of speeding cars. The urge to stay alive works so strongly, through so many aspects of our being, that we can sometimes overlook the tendency that ultimately overcomes it—the tendency to die. For a species to change and adapt, individuals must constantly reproduce and die off. For the form of life to persist, species need to mutate and change. Whereas, to the individual, death seems final and abrupt, it plays a necessary part in the perpetuation of life. In humans, death most naturally occurs through aging or disease. As we age, our bodies get less good at repairing and regenerating themselves. (For other species, predation can also play a significant role in mortality rates.) In species generally, the average life span tends to be as long as the species requires to persist and no longer.

Each of us represents the form of life, through our individual existence and through the part we play in passing on the human type from one generation to the next. At times, we apprehend this instinctively and immediately, experiencing a feeling of oneness with all living creatures. When we let go of our egos, our immediate sense of our selves, we can perceive life as a thing in itself, a form that never dies and never stops growing.

Similarly, if we can let go of our physical being, we can apprehend indirectly our place in the universe and the tendency to persist as it appears through matter—the galaxies, stars, and planets in whose swirling explosive grandeur we can still discern the enormous forces that gave rise to the universe: the scale and beauty of the oceans and mountains here on earth; the structure of crystals and rocks, their regularity and irregularity; the forces between fundamental particles and the way these forces give rise to all of the elements and molecules in everything we see and touch; the equivalence of energy and matter. We become aware that we form part of the universe; that we exist through the existence of the universe, not outside it; that all existence works in accordance with the same fundamental design—to be, to keep coming into being, to persist, and ultimately to cease to be, conforming with fundamental and immutable laws of causality that don't appear in space and time but shape the path and our perception of space and time.

Section 1: Understanding the Forms of Existence

Part 3—Understanding Consciousness

What Is Consciousness?

As I look through the window, I see smoke blowing away from the chimney stack of the house next door. I don't know that my neighbor has a fire burning in his grate, but I deduce that he has. To arrive at this conclusion, which at first seems elementary, I realize that I have worked subconsciously (or at least, I wasn't aware of any conscious process) through a number of concepts. I must have understood that the billowing gray wispiness above the neighboring chimney stack resembled the by-product of some burning carbon material. I must have rejected the possibility that the chimney stack itself was burning, because I can see that it is made of ceramic (which I know doesn't burn) and because I know that the chimney stack is designed to pass smoke up and out of the house from a fireplace below. And I must have then deduced that a fire had been started in the grate and that the person most likely to light a fire in the grate is my neighbor.

These mental formulations have happened instantaneously, apparently without any thought at all, the fluency and speed of the intervening steps making it hard to grasp at first that concepts are

at work. And how odd it is to attribute the process to the function-
ing of consciousness when my subconscious, it seems, has made all
the connections. But without the faculty of consciousness I could
not access these concepts, and my subconscious could not make
any of the connections. The nonconscious mind can only connect
smoke with fire through repeated experience and association rather
than through understanding a chain of cause and effect. An animal
may establish a link between a certain smell, the appearance of a
billowing gray cloud, and the sensation of intense heat by having
experienced these perceptions (always connected) before. But for a
nonconscious animal, there is no abstraction and subsequent conceptual interpretation.

Through mutation, living organisms developed brain functions that coordinated the processes of the body and its response to
external stimuli. Over time, these brain functions changed to allow
animals to discern and understand patterns and associations that
they could exploit to their advantage.

The lines between instinct, learned behavior, and conscious
thought can be fuzzy and difficult to draw. Sometimes what
appears to be conscious thought may be pure instinct or learned
behavior. Does the rabbit thump its hind legs in response to threat
instinctively or through an awareness that this will alert other rab-
bits to danger? Does the squirrel figure out that by hanging upside
down it can dislodge seed from the bird-feeder, or does the squirrel just do it, associate the behavior with reward, and repeat it?

Consciousness began as a mutation of brain function that
enabled the conscious organism to understand abstract form, rather
than continuing to work only through immediate impressions and
perceptions. The most immediate and fundamental impression of
all (before sight, sound, smell, touch, taste) is the impression of our
physical being, our sense of our own physicality. The first and fundamental concept is the differentiation of self from nonself.

The infant has no sense of nonself; the whole world merges
with its immediate perceptions. The baby reflects his pain or discomfort immediately and unrelentingly onto the world around him
by crying; he knows only instinct. But as the infant becomes aware
that he has a self and that this self is separate from the selves of his
mother and father—that the external world doesn't simply serve or

impinge on his senses—the child has conceived his first concept and entered the world of consciousness.

We keep one foot in both worlds throughout our lives. Almost everything we do involves some application of concepts either consciously or subconsciously, but at times what we perceive directly is so unfamiliar that we can't apply a concept in the moment. At other times, our immediate impressions obliterate our sense of the world around us; we feel something so strongly that our feelings swamp and submerge our conscious faculties (for instance, when we experience blind rage, abject fear, extreme pain, or pure wonder).

We form concepts through striving to make sense of our perceptions. Very often we work through ill-formed or erroneous concepts, but as individuals and as a species we tend to improve our conceptual understanding as we grow and learn. Understanding breeds understanding. Working from our perceptions, our minds seek an abstract model that will give a coherent, repeatable, and sensible mechanism for the appearance of the perception. A dog won't put its paw in a fire because the closer it moves the paw to the fire, the greater is its impression of pain and discomfort. Young children, we hope, will avoid fire for the same reason. But as a child gets older, she learns that the flame causes pain because it burns. What older child hasn't experimented with a candle flame, letting it graze her hand, having learned that, in order to burn, the flame must remain in contact with the skin for more than a split second. Or she may simply want to test the threshold between pain and her ability to master pain. The interaction of the child with the concepts of flame, burning, and pain become quite sophisticated and far removed from the original straightforward association of pain with the heat of the flickering orange light.

The earliest conscious organisms formed conceptual objects corresponding to the objects of their immediate perception—their senses (the direct objects of their experience), an aspect of consciousness that of course remains enormously powerful and important. Consciousness is not restricted to the objects of our immediate perception, however. Conceptual objects exist separate and distinct from the actual objects of perception and therefore are not limited to the actual objects of our perception.

For instance, I transform my immediate perception of the chair I'm sitting on into the concept of a chair. I experience the chair directly through its appearance, through my tactile sensation of its structure, even through its smell. I form certain ideas about my immediate perceptions and transform these into concepts relating to the color and texture of the chair; the material it's made of; its steadiness, size, weight. The conceptual object I hold before my mind's eye is not the same as the chair; it does not even directly mirror my immediate perceptions of the chair. (As Bertrand Russell points out in his 1912 *Problems of Philosophy*, I may think of the chair as uniformly brown, even though parts of it look white because of reflected light or black because of deep shadow. Under a range of conditions, the chair tends to reflect more brown light than it does other parts of the visible spectrum, so I simplify this in a kind of conceptual shorthand, labeling the chair as brown.) My consciousness fashions a simplified, coherent, and idealized mental representation of the chair. So long as my concept of the chair lets me usefully manipulate and interact with the conceptual object (for instance, allowing me to understand what will happen if I lean back in the chair, or to remember that this is my chair, or to describe it later so that someone else can find it), my conceptual object has served its purpose and needn't be more accurate.

The capacity to form and reflect on conceptual objects brings with it the capacity to conceive of that which we don't perceive. We can form and manipulate conceptual objects in ways that diverge from our immediate perceptions (I can imagine a chair without legs, or one made of asparagus). The chair doesn't have a particular color; the color I see varies across the surface of the chair and depending on the way the light reflects from its surface and depending on my viewpoint. And yet we all collect such perceptions into concepts of color of uniformity or generality that don't have any exact manifestation in the world around us. I apply the abstract concept of brown or gray to a chair, but when I say that the chair is brown or gray, I mean that my perception of its hue has a tendency toward general brownness or grayness. Similarly, we daily use concepts such as a straight line and a circle, even though the straight lines and circles that appear in the world around us are approximations (nothing in the material world is completely straight or completely circular). Concepts, on the other hand, can encompass and represent any aspect of the physical world.

Conceptual objects do not exist in the physical world and so have no limits or constraints; they are not beholden to the world of physical objects. This should not be disconcerting, although it is astounding and miraculous—conceptual existence doesn't require the objects of the real world but can reflect them and anticipate them. Consciousness is a sense just as sight and sound and smell and taste and touch are senses, but it responds to mental rather than physical stimuli, to conceptual rather than physical objects. Our immediate physical sensory perceptions inform our mental impulses but do not limit or define our mental impulses. The key to understanding consciousness therefore will come through a consideration of the mental process by which we manipulate conceptual objects.

Contribution of Consciousness to Tendencies toward Persistence

From the moment we wake up in the morning until the moment we go to sleep at night, we are continuously bringing the world of our perception under the reflection of our consciousness and making choices consistent with our conscious understanding of our perceptions. When I roll over in bed to check my clock, I put to use the concepts of space and causality (unless someone has moved it, I'll find the clock in the same place it sat when I went to sleep last night), the concept of time (if I know where I am in the continuum of moments, I'll know whether it's time to get up or not), the concept of human divisions of time (the hands on the clock will represent a particular point on the time continuum that society has agreed to measure in hours and minutes). Sometimes, as in this example, the application of a particular set of concepts can seem trivial or only remotely related to our persistence, and sometimes it can seem critically important—should I marry this person, should I have that operation...

As conscious beings, we have insight into the workings of the world around us, insight that is inaccessible to nonconscious organisms, and we can use this greater understanding to make choices that will tend to improve our chances of individual survival and successful reproduction. If I'm caught in a thunderstorm and lie down in a field to avoid acting as a lightning rod, I'm applying concepts of electrical energy and conduction to further my persistence. If we trade vegetables with our neighbors, we're using concepts of ownership and trade to further the persistence of our immediate social groups and the human species generally. If we vote for government leaders who will sign an environmental protection treaty, we're working through the concepts of a sustainable environment and mutual cooperation to further the persistence of life as a form. For the thinking creature, the process of thoughtful decision making plays a pervasive and critical role in persistence.

We can and do form concepts about any and every aspect of our existence and constantly work to manipulate these concepts to achieve an advantage for ourselves or others. Concepts so infuse our lives that we can find it hard to separate the conceptual objects from the perceptual objects. My mind immediately translates pangs of emptiness in my stomach into the concept of hunger. We extend the reproductive urge into the concept of sexual arousal. Consciousness infiltrates, informs, modifies, distorts (by error or approximation), clarifies, and enriches every aspect of our lives.

Although we do experience feelings, instincts, and urges directly, we tend to immediately bring them into consciousness. Other than pure, direct, instinctive acts and reflex actions (gasping for breath, jumping out of the path of an oncoming vehicle), our choices and actions come out of a complex interplay of that which we feel or experience directly and that which we have consciously processed. We don't eat as a nonconscious animal eats. We tend to modify the act of eating so that it conforms to a conscious model of eating; we wrap the act in concepts and ritual. We eat with utensils, from plates; we chew with our mouths closed. We typically don't have sex in immediate and direct response to the reproductive urge; instead, we tend to form a conscious awareness of the urge and how socially acceptable it may be to act on it in that moment. Unless we're overcome by rage, we tend not to simply attack others even when we have the urge to hurt them—conscious reflection modifies such impulses and leads us to restrain ourselves.

What's most important is that consciousness influences choice. Any choice to do or not do involves conscious reflection. As conscious beings, we can and do make choices that will affect our persistence and the persistence of other living organisms. A nonconscious animal doesn't think about the impact of its actions; it just acts. As conscious beings we have the capacity to weigh and assess the impacts of our choices on our own survival, the survival of our families or social groups, and even the survival of life as a form. And we have the capacity to consider how our actions may work in our favor while working against the interests of others. Consciousness gives us the power to choose for the general good, or to choose in accordance with our own self-interest. Morality, then, is a function of consciousness.

If we consider again the three aspects of the tendency to persist in the form of life—the individual, the particular type or species, and the form of life itself—we can see that only conscious organisms can choose to act solely in accordance with the third aspect. A nonconscious organism will instinctively tend to strive to further its own life and the life of its immediate social group or species, but only a conscious creature can be aware of and make choices consistent with the persistence of the form of life itself (choosing a course of action that doesn't serve the individual or the species but serves life as a form).

Imagine a bear trundling through the woods and coming across a baby bird, helpless without its mother. Would the bear rescue the bird? In a book or movie, perhaps, but not in the real world. In fiction, we imbue the bear that rescues the baby bird with the human quality of conscious awareness. Consciousness allows us to understand that we can and should contribute to the persistence of life as a form. Consciousness allows us to feel empathy for other living creatures, for their plight and struggle for survival, through an understanding that all species are varieties of the form of existence that is life.

Nonconscious creatures kill for food without hesitation—no selfless thought process could lead a tiger or lion to spare its victim. But for human beings, killing for food or allowing others to kill for food on our behalf can involve some degree of choice—some choose not to eat meat, for instance, because they do not believe in killing animals for food.

Although many concepts simply reflect the immediate objects of our perception (pain, hunger, the reproductive urge), allowing us to manipulate those objects, other concepts remove our choices and actions from the world of immediate and direct perception. These concepts, too, usually have some ground (even though it might be a false or flawed ground) in the immediate objects of our perception. For example, the concept of fashion, of dressing well and looking good, affects to a greater or lesser degree some choices we make in our everyday lives. The concept of fashion has its ground in the reproductive urge, in the desire to attract. The concept of government and law has at its ground the direct instinct to protect and preserve the individual and the broader social group. Of course, the concept of government can be distorted through bad government or bad law, but the ground lies in an awareness that through organization and order we will tend to further our persistence and the persistence of our family and friends.

As Schopenhauer noted, conscious beings can choose to willfully destroy life. We have the option to work against our persistence, or the persistence of others. For this reason, Schopenhauer decided that consciousness was anomalous and not part of the universal striving to be. In this Schopenhauer erred, however. Consciousness evolved according to exactly the same principles of existence as those that brought about material existence and life in all its variations. We have no reason to see consciousness as operating outside the universal rules. Though consciousness creates the possibility of choices and acts that willfully work against the tendency to persist, so, too, can a virus or predator blindly work against the tendency to persist. Consciousness and the world of concepts makes it possible for conscious creatures to improve their persistence. But consciousness also comes with the possibility that conscious choices may jeopardize life in some or all of its variations. A particular mutation does not guarantee adaptation and improved persistence, but merely the possibility for adaptation.

* * * * *

We have arrived at an understanding of the principle of persistence in inanimate matter and the form of life by observing existence, by discerning its nature. The process of demonstrating this principle and how it reveals itself has been somewhat painstaking. Now that we're on the subject of consciousness, however, we should note that the principle of persistence is not some vague, remote concept. We experience the urge to persist directly, and we understand this concept through and through—so instinctively and deeply that it has been difficult for us to root it out. The concept behind the principle appears immediately and dramatically when something threatens our lives or the lives of those we care about. "I want to live," it says, "I want others to live."

Consciousness allows us to grasp any and all concepts; this ability is limited only by intellectual capacity. Theoretically, with a complete grasp of all concepts and sufficient desire for persistence, we can consistently make choices that avoid harm to life as a form. As a species, though, we have not yet attained a sufficiently sophisticated understanding of existence to avoid the possibility of self-destruction. (Again, mutation acts blindly. The birth of consciousness did not anticipate biological weapons, nuclear bombs, the depletion of the planet's natural resources, pollution, genocide. Our consciousness endangers the persistence of humankind and possibly life on earth, despite its having brought us medicines, agriculture, conservation, charity, and conscience.)

Are we improving? Taking a historical perspective, despite glaring and terrible examples to the contrary, we tend to be more aware than our ancestors of the importance of kindness, tolerance, and empathy in improving our general chances of survival as a species and the survival of life as a form.

Consciousness and the Inanimate

As conscious beings, we can see through the outward and immediate appearance of material existence to the concepts behind it. We experience beauty in form and appropriateness in function. The arc of a shooting star and the crest of a wave hold conceptual meaning and weight—from the star's trajectory we infer the concept of attenuation and curvature, in the wave's peak and fall we sense the concept of a boundary between the drive of upward momentum and the tug of gravity, the exquisite moment of turning back and dropping down, the chaotic tumult of the foaming water. Nonconscious creatures do not experience any of this wonder and beauty, which we access only through an awareness of the concepts at work.

We perceive many of the conceptual objects that relate to physical existence (such as shape, consistency, hue) and we perceive many of the conceptual objects that relate to causal relationships (friction, collision, succession, simultaneity, momentum, variation). Through these perceptions, we experience an appreciation for the elegance and appropriateness of function of the concepts that govern physical existence.

The concepts of mathematics and science derive from translating our perception of the world of physical existence into a model for the rules governing physical existence. Mathematics has its basis in the concept of causality; we experience mathematics directly and in a binary sense through the separation of self from nonself. This simple starting point proceeds naturally and beautifully into the systems of natural numbers, fractions, algebra, fractals, and differential calculus. The more we understand about the concepts that reflect the world around us, the more we appreciate that the ridges in our fingernails follow similar patterns similar to the ridges of sand on a beach, or the ripples of diffracted light above a heat haze. Our conscious awareness and understanding of the physical world lead us ultimately to the conclusion that we are one with the rest of physical existence, that our sense of separation is illusory.

Section 2: Understanding Universal Concepts

Classes of Concepts

I'm sitting in my wife's office today, reinstalling software on her new computer while I write. Usually I work upstairs, looking out over the city. If I let my imagination wander for a moment, I can imagine that the house has floors above and below the floors I know to exist. In my mind's eye, the floors above and below rise and sink indefinitely, each new upper floor with a more spectacular view of the city than the one below it, each new subbasement with a more dingy claustrophobic feel than the one above. I know that these objects of my imagination do not exist, could not exist in reality (we could maybe add a couple of floors before surpassing practical limits of engineering), but my imagination can summon and grasp these concepts firmly and with ease.

Conceptual objects, unlike material physical objects, need not conform to any constraints or bounds. A conscious being can conceive of any concept, whether it represents the objects of perception or not. Some things can be more difficult to conceive of than others, and certainly since the range of concepts is infinite, many concepts have not been conceived of, although this doesn't mean they could not be.

The range and dexterity of the conscious mind come as no surprise if we consider that forming even the simplest of concepts requires a surprising degree of abstraction from our direct perceptions. To understand a chair, we need to reflect on the image and sensation of the physical object from different perspectives. We need to consider the chair's geometry. When we look at it from one side or another, or from the top or the bottom, we must make allowances for the distortion of perspective and viewing angle, the variation in the brightness and hue of reflected light. We can then discern the sensation of sitting on the chair, moving our weight forward and back or from side to side. And we synthesize these observations into the concept of a solid object with a substantial platform on which a person can sit more or less securely without tipping off under a normal range of motion. The concept of a chair, therefore, requires considerable abstraction and the interplay between a whole host of concepts. Only after this process of abstraction can it be held before the consciousness in an ideal form.

We can use the example of a chair to illustrate how a discussion of concepts can easily become difficult and confused. If we have only ever encountered four-legged chairs, we may limit the concept of a chair to something with four legs supporting a platform that a person can sit on. Or, to restate, in a world where only four-legged chairs exist, we attach the word *chair* to the concept of a four-legged sitting structure. Now, if in this world someone conceived of a sitting structure with only three legs, the idea would require either a new word to represent that concept or extension of the meaning of *chair* to encompass the three-legged sitting structure. From the perspective of the world of concepts, however, the concept of a three-legged sitting structure didn't suddenly come into being. Rather, in the class of all concepts (which includes not just three-legged but also two-legged, one-legged, and no-legged chairs, whether anyone had conceived of these or not), the concept of a three-legged chair has moved from the subclass of those objects that hadn't been conceived of, and into a subclass of possible, real, or existing objects. While this example is trivial and artificial, the very human and understandable process of misapplying or mistakenly limiting concepts has caused and continues to cause many real and sometimes tremendous difficulties and problems.

To use a more pertinent and pragmatic difficulty, the concepts we understand by use of the terms *fetus*, *unborn child*, and *human life* differ, depending on our perspective and the way in which we understand these terms and related concepts. Our differences on abortion reflect our differences in processing the concepts impinging on our religious and moral beliefs and values. These are not differences of terminology, as they were in the case of the three-legged sitting structure, but differences of conceptual perspective.

Everything we can bring to mind is a conceptual object: our perceptions of physical objects, rules of mathematics, logical and illogical deductions, imaginary beings, recollections of dreams, assignations of good and evil. Some conceptual objects correspond to direct perceptions (such as the concept of the chair's being sat on), some correspond to our indirect perceptions (rules of arithmetic and theories of physics), others correspond neither to our direct perceptions nor to our indirect perceptions, even though they may be closely related to or derived from them.

Although conceptual objects know no restriction in scope and no limitation in number or variation, certain classes or categories of conceptual objects bear more directly than others on our experience of the world around us. We can define a superclass of these classes—the class of conceptual objects that contributes to our understanding of existence.

Defining a class of conceptual objects that contribute to our understanding of existence provides a useful if amorphous distinction. History provides innumerable examples of conceptual objects once thought to represent existence with complete accuracy, only to be found inadequate (Newton's theory of gravity, for instance, which was supplanted by Einstein's general relativity). If a concept applies even empirically and under constrained conditions, however, we can use it to inform our choices in the world. Newtonian gravity applies perfectly adequately in the nonrelativistic realm; an understanding of Newtonian gravity is more useful than no concept of gravity.

Of particular importance is the class of pure concepts—concepts that correspond to immutable and fully consistent functions or principles (as opposed to approximations). Fundamental to this class of conceptual objects are the concepts of space, time, and causality. These conceptual objects correspond to our indirect perception of the physical universe, its extension and duration in time, and the underlying laws or principles that delimit the ways in which the various aspects of the physical universe can interact. The purity of these concepts rests on one assumption—that the universe exists and is not an illusion.

We may not know or understand the class of pure concepts in its entirety, but if we accept that existence is real and not illusory, then we know that such a class exists. As a member of this class, a concept reflects the true nature of an aspect of existence rather than an approximation. These concepts have the greatest value to us in understanding existence. The more certain we can be about the purity of a particular concept, the more we can apply it success-fully. (Although we can derive great value from the concept of "two plus two usually equals four," we can derive more value from the concept of "two plus two always equals four.")

The superclass of concepts that contributes to our under-standing of existence, then, includes the following three sub-classes:

1. The class of conceptual objects that represents the world of our direct perception (sensation of physical self, sen-sation of mental self, sensation of physical objects that we observe in the world around us—the class that corre-sponds to Schopenhauer's "world as representation," meaning our limited and constrained direct experience of the universe)

2. The class of conceptual objects that represents approxi-mate models corresponding to the world of our direct perception (all of the empirical laws of science, such as Newtonian gravity, animal behavior and psychology, and human psychology)

3. The class of conceptual objects that represents the pure ideas of the world of our direct and indirect perception (time, space, geometry, arithmetic, causality)

Through our direct perceptions, we interact with and have an awareness of the universe. Over time, as we analyze and synthesize our direct perceptions, we expand our knowledge and understand-ing of the other two classes. We use this knowledge and under-standing to gain greater control over the world around us, to reduce and eliminate uncertainty. We use our knowledge and understanding to help us persist.

The class of approximate models gives us power over our immediate surroundings. It helps us predict the outcome of our actions. By understanding and applying a good model of reality, we can fashion tools and machines, navigate using a compass, give comfort to a friend. But the approximate or representative concept will always have limits to its usefulness. Newtonian gravity applies under certain conditions and within certain tolerances, and if we use it to explain or predict phenomena in the relativistic realm, we get the wrong results. Models based on empirical observation will always be open to refinement and replacement.

The class of pure ideas, on the other hand, does not suffer these limitations. Conceptually speaking, one plus one will always and by definition equal two. The shortest distance between two points will always be a straight line. We can therefore exert the most control over our surroundings and eliminate the most uncertainty if we can apply pure concepts whenever and wherever possible.

Over the course of human history, we have (for the most part) consistently and systematically worked to expand the grounds and range of our understanding of these classes of concepts. We have tended to move in the direction of gaining a more complete understanding, with a few glaring examples to the contrary. These steps forward often get a merciless and hostile reception; reactionary members of society will resist and try to suppress new understanding. Revolutionary thinking can scare us or threaten the status quo. However, human society tends to ultimately absorb new ideas.

In the United States in recent years we have witnessed a remarkable and distressing example of a local reversal of this general trend—fundamentalist Christians' refusal to accept the concept of evolution. This kind of backward step can seem alarming and indeed is alarming for those who suffer as a result of it, but we can expect that this anomalous and perplexing regression will eventually right itself. Members of a group that adopts a creationist perspective will tend to do poorly in competition with those who acknowledge the limitations of this perspective. To return to the example of a chair: if I understand the concept of chairness, I can benefit from that understanding by sitting. Likewise, if I understand the concept of evolution, I can benefit from that understanding by evolving.

In his short story "The Library of Babel" (*Ficciones*, 1944), Jorge Luis Borges—a master of conceptual exploration—imagines a library that contains every book ever written and every book that could ever be written. Here can be found books that differ by only one word or one letter, and books that contain nothing but consonants. As the story unfolds, we begin to sense the infinite horror and impossibility of such a library. But Borges's image captures the universe of concepts and their classification. Concepts are infinitely varied, infinitely malleable, infinitely divisible and gradable. We could fill an infinite number of shelves with all of the possible ways that concepts can be defined and classified.

Through scientific, mathematical, and logical analysis, many of the concepts important to us as human beings have been clearly and cleanly defined—the physical composition and interaction of objects, geometry, proof by induction. And although some concepts still elude our full understanding, in most cases we're aware of the approach to finding our way to such an understanding. But certain important concepts that affect our everyday lives in significant ways have evaded our understanding for centuries, despite the best efforts of some of the best minds of each era. Philosophers and theologians have struggled to find an absolute ground for morality; some still think there is none. Entire nations spent much of the last century in a state of war or standoff over political ideological differences, fascism or communism versus democracy, a dispute over the pure ground for good government. And despite the continuing daily production of countless works of art, despite the revered life works of painters, writers, sculptors, composers, we share no common understanding of what makes good art and what doesn't. Do the concepts of morality, ethics, and beauty have a pure basis? And if so, can we discern that pure basis, bringing human understanding to a new level?

Morality as a Conceptual Object

How does my daughter learn right from wrong, good from

bad? Certainly she receives direct and indirect instruction from me and from her stepmother, her mother, her schoolteachers, and her peers. Even books and movies provide her with moral insight. But how does she make sense of conflicting lessons, confusing points, misdirection; how does she abstract from the haphazard particular examples to the bigger picture? Is it possible that we instinctively understand the difference between right and wrong, regardless of instruction or misinstruction?

Dorothy, who turned twelve this year, seems to understand many moral concepts. She makes her way in the moral world fairly independently, arriving at decisions and assessments of good and bad without seeming to have much difficulty. Moral sensibilities are at work in children much younger than twelve. I remember Dorothy as a moral being at age two or three, showing concern and empathy, being aware of modes of behavior. The first glimmers of her sense of morality appeared as she began to separate her sense of self from her sense of the rest of the world—in other words, that her sense of morality apparently arrived with consciousness.

Do we, as conscious organisms, have an innate ability to perceive an absolute moral frame of reference, a pure basis for morality that we perceive as we would any other pure concept, like near and far, big and small? And does this framework appear with consciousness or exist before it?

It was Plato who first directly tackled, and attacked, the notion that our perception of good and bad, right and wrong, justice and injustice, courage and cowardice may be absolute. He recognized that we typically assume that we know good from bad, and he then set about exploring and dismantling the basis for this sense of confidence. In his Socratic dialogs, Plato pits the moral certainty of the learned and prominent men of ancient Greece against Socrates' unremitting skepticism. Invariably, Socrates' interlocutor starts out by asserting quite confidently that he can define goodness or justice, only to be left confounded or angered by Socrates' methodical demonstration that his moral concepts rest on subjective rather than objective grounds.

Implicit in Plato's Socratic refutation of moral absolutes, however, seems to be a nagging awareness that goodness and justice may indeed be founded on some pure conceptual basis. Everyone (except Socrates) seems to readily accept and defend the proposition that such a conceptual basis must exist, whether he can define it or not, and whether or not he agrees with his fellow citizens on its application in the particular. Plato seems to be saying that the concept of goodness certainly exists, but an absolute ground that can be rigorously defined and applied eludes us.

* * * * *

Some say that morality rests on a clear and unambiguous interpretation of a particular religious text (the Bible or the Torah or the Koran) and that we should define *good* and *bad* by a correspondence to or deviation from the teachings of the text; for these believers, morality rests on the pure concept of correspondence. But immediately we have a problem: The text in question has been interpreted (and inevitably modified through that interpretation).

More important (and pragmatic), the text came after millennia of human existence; humans understood good and bad for thousands of years before it was written. We want to know why children or atheists or agnostics (or believers in other religions) still have a sense of good and bad, right and wrong. Surely, religious texts transcribe in one way or another an interpretation of an instinctive sense of morality, not the other way around.

Can we found an absolute morality on human laws? Human laws can be understood and applied definitively. But leaving aside the obvious problem that legislation is littered with bad laws, human laws proceed from our innate sense of right and wrong, not the other way around.

If we want to find an absolute point of reference for good and bad, right and wrong, we will have to look for it where it appears and find out why it appears. We encounter moral choices and seek to apply moral judgments in the situations that face us in the world of existence. Every moral choice has some reference to material existence and to the living world. Therefore, any moral basis will appear through an understanding of material existence and life.

An organism without consciousness acts instinctively. It is impossible for a nonconscious animal to make moral choices— such an animal does not have access to concepts and therefore does not have an awareness of goodness or badness. To put it another way: every choice a nonconscious animal makes is guided by instinct, experience, and circumstance and is therefore its only available choice. A conscious organism, on the other hand, can conceptualize his instincts and experiences, and make choices guided by those concepts. Morality—the assessment of good and bad—is a conscious process and only a conscious process.

When we refer to the concepts of good and bad in a particular situation, what are we trying to determine? If we think again about nonconscious organisms, it is much easier to understand the principle that guides their actions. Existence, persistence: the form of life relies on the premise that an animal will typically act in ways that benefit its persistence or the persistence of its family or community. As conscious organisms, we use concepts of good and bad to help guide our actions, a process that simply extends the nonconscious process. The hungry wolf sees a sheep in the pasture and, acting according to the principle of persistence, attacks. The hungry man sees apples in his neighbor's orchard and feels the impulse to pluck one and eat it. But when he pauses and brings this impulse under the scrutiny of his consciousness, he now weighs the desire to pick an apple and eat it against the damage this might cause to his relationship with his neighbor. This conscious process doesn't invoke a new and different principle; on the contrary, it extends and refines the same principle.

The hungry man's desire not to annoy or betray the trust of his neighbor rests on the same fundamental ground as his desire to eat the apple. In both cases, he concerns himself with the persistence of life as a form. Through his impulse to pluck the apple, he encounters the principle of persistence in its immediate form as it applies to him as an individual—to assuage his hunger, to feed himself, to live. In not wishing to anger or upset his neighbor, he encounters the principle again: he wishes to protect himself from retribution and to protect his mutually beneficial relationship with his neighbor.

Morality, then, rests on the fundamental principle of animate existence, an aspect of life that is constant, universal, and unchanging—that which tends to persist will tend to exist. That which contributes to our persistence, or the persistence of our species, or the persistence of life as a form is definitively better than that which does not. Contribution to persistence is good, detriment to persistence is bad. Morality is the conscious reflection of life's opportunistic striving to continue to exist. All moral concepts derive from our intuitive or conceptual understanding of the principle of persistence.

The three-year-old already has a sense that she lives and that other organisms live, and an intuitive and innate awareness that this sense of existence derives from an actual existence. She knows without needing to think about it that if she were to cease to exist, she would stop being aware of her existence. As living organisms, we experience nonbeing as anathema. Life exists to exist. Because the conscious child exists as a living organism and knows of no other possible form of existence, she experiences her continued persistence as essential and positive.

Moral sensibility arrives with the apprehension of self. The first moral imperative instructs us simply to continue to persist. As we become aware that each person has a self that calls on that person to persist, we cast a wider moral net. And when we realize that our human self selves are a variation of the living form, our moral awareness expands to encompass the impact of our actions on all living things. The three-year-old wishes for her parents and siblings and cats and dogs and goldfish to persist, and she makes choices consistent with this desire. The child understands intuitively the essential goodness of the continued existence of life as a form.

As we mature and grow, we attain a more subtle, nuanced, and relative appreciation of the concepts of right and wrong, good and bad. We have to weigh and assess our sense of that which will tend to contribute to our own persistence against that which will contribute to the persistence of others, or to life in general. Faced with the choice of taking the last donut or leaving it for someone else, a child comes up against his first moral dilemma—does he act in his own interests or the interests of others?

Because the persistent tendency in living organisms operates through the individual, the group or type, and the form of life itself, we need to look to all three to understand how they complement and (more important) constrain one another when we make moral choices:

- That which tends to work in favor of the persistence of the individual, but against the persistence of the group or species, can be defined as bad. Similarly, that which works, overall, in favor of the persistence of the group or type—even though it may work against the persistence of a particular individual—must be considered good. (Without the continued existence of the species, the continued existence of the individual is irrelevant.) The boy who leaves the last donut for his friends does more to further the species than the boy who takes the last donut for himself.
- That which tends to work in favor of the persistence of the group or type, but against the persistence of life as a form, can be defined as bad. And that which tends overall to work in favor of the persistence of the form of life itself, but against the persistence of a particular group, species or individual, can be defined as good.

The skeptical reader might argue that a definition of morality that rests on persistence still relies on subjective and relative distinctions, at best, and operates crudely and coldly, at worst. If goodness calls merely for contribution to persistence, what about spirituality, what about sacrifice, what about enlightenment? But if for a moment we suspend our outrage, if we sit with this sense of goodness and consider how it might reflect and readily absorb the immediacy of our shared instincts and the richness of our real moral concerns, we start to see that it is only as relative, crude, and mistaken as we make it.

First of all, the definition gives us a pure, rigorous, and absolute conceptual ground from which to begin any moral discourse. If we choose in favor of the persistence of life as a form we act rightly; if we choose against the continued persistence of life as a form we act wrongly. The relativity and subjectivity arise in figuring out whether a particular choice will tend to contribute to persistence or not. This points to the complexity and subtlety of the different perspectives on what will contribute to persistence rather than to a flaw in the definition itself. The definition tells us what to aim for in arriving at our moral choices, not what they will be.

If we consider some simple examples, we start to see that the definition of an absolute morality grounded in the persistence of life as a form seems immediately and intuitively right:

- It is good to protect ourselves from danger (persistence in the individual).
- It is good to nurture and protect our loved ones (persistence in the group or species).
- It is bad to destroy another living organism solely for the sake of its destruction (persistence of life as a form).

Furthermore, because the concept of persistence derives from the concepts of time and arithmetic, both of which we understand as pure concepts, morality rests on a pure conceptual ground. The persistence of one entity in comparison to that of another entity can be understood through the concept of duration in time and the concept of relation (lasting longer—a comparison of the scale of one value to the scale of another). Morality asks what will lead to greater persistence of the living form. By defining goodness through the concept of persistence, we have brought it under the class of pure concepts. We have uncovered the absolute basis of morality.

Again, our moral understanding will only be as good as our understanding of how to apply the pure concept. Having an absolute basis for morality doesn't mean that suddenly all moral dilemmas will have obvious and definitive answers. (To demonstrate this by analogy, we can use an example from arithmetic, perhaps the most obviously pure concept. Without access to a powerful calculator or computer, even straightforward mathematical problems can defeat us—can we calculate in our heads the product of two one-hundred-digit numbers? Some mathematical problems have infinite solutions—for instance, elaborating the precise numerical value of an irrational number such as pi. We can't solve all mathematical problems just because mathematics rests on pure concepts. We need to be able to bring the particulars of each problem under our understanding in order to apply the concepts at work.) Once we can define morality as a pure concept, however, we can clarify our understanding of straightforward moral questions, removing them from the realm of subjectivity or opinion, and we can agree on a framework for the investigation and elaboration of more complex moral questions. If we accept that morality derives from the impact of a choice or action on the persistence of life as a form, all other moral frameworks must now be subject to reexamination and testing; they should no longer just be taken as given, or accepted on faith.

Of course, I say "if" we accept this. I am fully aware that many will refute the reasoning that brought us to this point. And many more will dismiss a nonspiritual basis for morality. This new understanding will be tested and defied, as have other theories that we now find indispensable.

Ethics, Government, and Justice as Conceptual Objects

The Roman emperor Claudius came to power in the wake of the bloody assassination of Julius Caesar. The conspirators who plotted Caesar's death had been dismayed by his abuse of power, his assumption of honors reserved for gods. Claudius, a quiet and studious man who had suffered ridicule for his physical infirmities throughout his life, favored a democratic republic over a monarchy. He had witnessed the corrosive influence of absolute power and the abuse of that power by his relatives since the relatively benign reign of his grandfather Augustus, and he well understood the benefit of a more democratic political form. Against his reservations, however, Claudius was persuaded to take on the role of emperor to maintain order and prevent unrest. He fully intended to give up the seat once things settled down.

Claudius went on to reign until his death thirteen years later, each year becoming more embroiled in his plans to improve the state of the empire. Each year, he pushed back his planned abdication. Once he saw the good that he could do—and the more convinced he became that without him his plans couldn't succeed—the less he wanted to step down. Claudius achieved many good things for Rome and for the empire, but eventually he too succumbed to the excesses of such a powerful position.

All organized societies require systems of ethics, government, and justice. Without such systems, a society cannot function as a society, but only as a loose collection of individuals. A system of organization provides a contract between the individual members of a society. This contract can be formal or informal, but whatever its form, it establishes an expectation of the way the society will operate. These systems can and do vary vastly in their extent and nature. Each nation must define some form of constitution and establish laws that codify the expectations of its citizens. A smaller community or group will follow a similar model, agreeing on the rules by which members must operate in order to remain part of the group. The social systems of royal courts go to the extent of stipulating how and when courtiers will address one another and who will sit first at the table, whereas the society of children in a schoolyard adheres to few absolute rules and tends to be very dynamic and flexible.

In a free society, a member can choose to accept or not accept the contract, to stay or to leave. But in a society that places constraints on its members, erecting barriers against exit, this contract may not be optional.

As the emperor Claudius recognized, the systems by which societies constitute and govern themselves tend to be imperfect. Claudius saw the value in establishing the rule of law. He embarked on projects that served the general good. Yet although he held fast to republican values, he ruled as a monarch, and eventually that absolute power corrupted even Claudius.

Ethics, government, and justice share a conceptual ground similar to the ground we've set out for morality—uncorrupted ethical, governmental, and judicial impulses rest on society's desire to further its persistence. (As with morality, no real-world systems of ethics, government, and justice can be perfect, since the application of the ground requires the application of judgment and the weighing of subtle shades of fairness and equity.)

Rules of ethics aim to guide the behavior of the members of society toward fairness and honesty and away from deception and cheating. This impulse rests on the concept of trust. Fair and equitable practices garner trust. With trust, we can proceed more quickly and with greater assurance of success toward forming contracts and partnerships. We can get on with things without worrying unduly that someone will cheat us. We will spend our energies on production rather than protection. And we will avoid the destructive influence of unfairness, of deception. The ground of this impulse, then, rests on the concept that ethical behavior will further the persistence of society. We will tend to have more chance of contributing to our own persistence (making a living), our family's persistence, and therefore society's persistence if we act ethically and can rely on others to act ethically. The society that can operate with a high degree of mutual trust tends to reap greater rewards from the labors of its members, to be more competitive, and to last longer by reducing or eliminating the destructive influences of deception and duplicity.

Societies institute governments to organize and oversee the operation of aspects of public affairs in which the community holds a common interest. Implicitly or explicitly, a society recognizes that through establishing government, society as a whole will benefit and prosper. Good government recognizes the needs of society, disseminates good ideas, establishes guidelines that will serve the general good, and creates an environment that supports productive individual and group pursuits while suppressing or eliminating generally harmful or destructive pursuits. Good government serves the purpose of society's persistence—maintaining that which society values, and furthering that which will help society prosper.

In contrast, poor governments tend to work against the persistence of the society being governed. Once the peoples of the communist countries in Eastern Europe began to feel that their governments didn't serve the general good, that individual freedoms were being unduly constrained, the seeds of communism's fall had been sown. The core principles of communism conform quite well to the idea that government should serve society's persistence, and the positive aspects of communism (and socialism) can be enormous—individuals feel invested in and part of the greater good, connected to and caring for their neighbors and society generally. But communism places such an emphasis on the general good at the expense of individual determinism that the balance can easily swing against the regime. Add to this the ideological impulse underlying communist principles—that communism is the only correct form of societal organization—and the corrupting tendency of power concentrated in the party's ruling elite, and we see that communist government does not tend to contribute as well as it might to the persistence of the society itself, nor to the persistence of life as a form.

Democracy aims to represent society's will by investing its members with a voice in choosing who will govern and how they will govern. A well-functioning democracy creates a dynamic mechanism by which society can monitor its own persistence and adjust as necessary. The flaw of democracy as a system of government lies in the difficulty that, when it comes time to vote, a significant proportion of the population must understand the complex matters of good government, social policy, fiscal management, and international diplomacy in order to elect the most appropriate leader. In most cases, the campaign slogans, superficial debates, mud-slinging, and character assassinations of modern politics obscure the issues, which in any case are too complex for even some politicians to grasp. Despite this flaw, any other form of government seems to be more flawed. The risk of any nondemocratic form of government lies in the corruptive influence of power, the risk that the wrong person or group will assume control and govern with narrow or destructive ends in mind.

Effective judicial systems provide guidance and control over the acts and actions of a society's members in such a way that society generally can operate safely and securely. Justice seeks to ensure society's persistence by monitoring and constraining the harmful or potentially harmful behavior of a society's citizens. Such constraints range from establishing murder (the most immediately drastic act against an individual's persistence) as a crime to creating laws that control what citizens can and can't do with a nation's symbols, such as flags or currency. (The argument for sanctions for acts against national symbols rests on the understanding that such acts work against persistence by threatening the shared convictions that hold the society together. The argument against sanctions for such actions states that such laws restrain the rights of society's members to free expression.)

Ethics, government, and law then overlap with morality because they share a common ground, but they are not one and the same. Morality, as we've established, has an absolute ground in the persistence of life as a form. Ethics, government, and law, on the other hand, stop short of an interest in the persistence of life as a form. Instead, they focus on the persistence of society. Ethics, government, and justice tend to resist forces that might lead to dramatic changes in the culture or operation of a particular society, even if those changes might serve life as a form. A society's rules and institutions tend to be set up to protect it from outside influences such as unrestricted commerce with other societies, cultural invasions, broad changes in demographics, revolutionary ideas, or new ways of working, not because these influences have been judged to work against the persistence of human life generally or as a whole, but because they work against the persistence of the particular society.

The tension between absolute morality and the pragmatic workings of ethical, governmental, and judicial concepts leads to many of the world's perennial problems and conflicts between communities, whether those communities are separated by ideology, geography, commerce, culture, or belief. To remain safe and secure, a particular society or group will tend to defend itself against the possibility of abrupt or uncontrolled change of any form or the possibility of attack—the self-interest of society focuses on its persistence. And so we have bigotry, racism, religious intolerance, invasion and counterinvasion, colonialism, repression, genocide, and war.

Beauty as a Conceptual Object

From where I sit I can see paintings on the walls, photographs of my son and daughter and wife, an antique cast iron stove (now an umbrella stand), various pieces of old furniture, a wooden mantle, a few potted plants, a computer, a stereo system. Music fills the room. In these narrow confines I am confronted by a wide spectrum of beauty. Someone else walking into the room might not share my perspective on the beauty of the objects. They might say that they don't like the look of the old stove, for example, that it's too pot-bellied or inelegant. Does this difference of opinion condemn beauty to the subjective realm? Or could we agree on an absolute basis for determining beauty even though our opinions on it vary?

Under the concept of beauty, I place anything that relates to perceived goodness or attractiveness of form, including aesthetic beauty (of natural or human-made objects), artistic beauty (in fine arts, poetry, music, literature, and so on), and intrinsic conceptual elegance (as in mathematical proofs). As with morality, we have an intuitive sense that beauty does rest on a pure basis. We dispute particular instances of beauty, but we all sense that beauty has a concrete ground; we instinctively feel that we have not just arrived at some collective illusion of such a quality.

A sense of beauty seems to arrive with a sense of self, with the development of consciousness and the apprehension of concepts. A child who stares in wonder at the falling snow, mouth open and eyes wide, experiences beauty in the profusion of descending white shadows, the tingling impacts on his face and the cool pricks as each flake hits his tongue. He witnesses the beauty without knowing the word *beauty*, without being told that this can be beautiful.

If I look at the pot-bellied stove with a more discerning eye, I admit that I don't particularly like the overall proportions, especially the arc of the upper torso. But I do like the classic lines of the lid, the solidity of the cast iron, and the evocation of a bygone time. We have fragile beauty, poems that laud fleeting feelings, art that represents the achingly ugly with such sensitive perception that it elevates and uplifts; we have the beauty of the infinite or the spiritual.

When the child gazes in awe at the falling snow, we can imagine that he perceives the unexpectedness of the experience; in his short life, nothing like this has happened before. The completeness and continuousness of the snowfall enthrall him, fill the world around him; and this immense and overwhelming change in his environment juxtaposes with the delicacy and softness and transience of the snowflakes themselves. Although he doesn't reflect on these concepts, he perceives them.

When we register something as beautiful, then, we respond to underlying concepts as they appear through the object of our perception. I appreciate the lines of the stove because I'm aware of the conceptual elegance of the geometry of the curves. The child, perceiving beauty in the falling snow, has subconsciously gathered the concepts of newness, of difference, of delicate coldness, of softness with tingling. These concepts impress him with their lightness and playfulness, with their overwhelming suddenness.

Appreciation of beauty does not require reflection, although it requires a direct apprehension of concepts. As conscious beings, we possess an innate and intuitive appreciation of concepts. We can perceive beauty without being able to explain it, because we directly perceive a relationship to an underlying concept. But we can also analyze our perception and articulate an explanation for our appreciation of a particular aspect of beauty.

If we define beauty as a direct or indirect correspondence to an underlying or related concept, we can see that beauty has a pure ground, correspondence being a pure concept. Again, as with morality, an assessment of beauty will tend to be relative, even though the ground is pure. Two people will not necessarily agree on the beauty of an experience because they won't necessarily experience it in relation to the same concepts.

To use a straightforward example, a poem using metaphors of snow and ice will tend to be perceived differently by someone who has no direct experience of snow and ice than by the person who lives in the frozen north. The concepts indirectly evoked by the metaphors in the poem will vary depending on whether the reader has ever stepped through the thin crust of ice lying atop the elusive white powder beneath.

Beauty can appear through relation to any concept. When we perceive beauty in natural objects (rocks, trees, flowers, running water), we perceive the forces and processes of existence. We can directly discern the beauty in the ripples on a body of water because we respond directly to the regularity of the appearance of the peaks and troughs arising through wave motion, the implicit sinusoidal shape of the waves that we discern through the gradients in reflected light, and the gradual diminishing of the wave amplitude as the ripples subside—a poignant echo of the tendency toward entropy. And yet we can discern the beauty of ripples on a body of water without any of these explicit references passing through our consciousness. We have a direct and innate appreciation for the forces of existence because we exist, and because existence comes about through the consistent application of a set of pure concepts (as we've discussed previously).

Architectural beauty arises out of a relationship of structure to form; the pure concepts of mathematics and physics can give rise to a building that has beautiful proportions and shape. The architect works with a set of lines that relate to concepts of straightness or arc, to the concepts of angles and relationships between lengths, guiding our apprehension of mathematical concepts through these lines. She also works with principles of engineering. We appreciate the apparent mass of the elements of the structure, how the mass is distributed and supported. She works with light and shadow, with our sense of scale and space. Architectural beauty therefore typically arises out of pure concepts. But it can also arise from artificial or imaginary concepts (gargoyles, for instance, do not reflect a pure concept).

Much modern architecture (and modern art) aims to create something of beauty through deliberately subverting our expected sense of what architecture should be, by striving to create a relationship to abstract concepts. A building that seems to defy gravity or is constructed of materials that don't conform to our expectation of what a building should be made of might generate feelings of unease and surprise in those who come across it. These feelings correspond to the architect's intent to express difference from and defiance of familiar and expected architecture. Individuals disagree on the effectiveness of such experiments, on the beauty of the results, because we apprehend and respond differently to the concepts at work in the design.

The degree of beauty doesn't relate to the concept being represented, although a better or more effective correspondence may be perceived as more beautiful. And if we understand the class of concepts being represented, we can better understand why something is beautiful. With art that aims to illuminate abstract concepts, we need a conscious appreciation of those concepts before we can arrive at a full appreciation of the beauty of the work. In modern art, we may be lost without an understanding of what the artist intended.

We can define art as a creative act inspired by the impulse to represent and communicate a perceived concept. Artists seek to unearth and represent their perception of concepts. This definition may seem to exclude paintings, compositions, sculptures, and other art in the creation of which the artists simply sought to paint, write, or sculpt what they observed, where they had no communication of concept in mind. Purely mechanical painting, composition or sculpture—an exercise solely in technique—seeks only to represent the individual's fluency with that technique. In other words, art cannot be simply a display of technique, unless the artist elevates the display of technique to a concept—postmodernism in literature provides an example of this. On the other hand, any painting, composition, sculpture, or other art that emerges without any conscious desire to communicate perspective, and without being an exercise solely in technique, nevertheless communicates a subconscious perception of concepts. Whether conscious or not, art derives from the urge to respond to a concept.

Section 3: Understanding Morality

Objective Morality

If I draw three straight lines on a piece of paper, with both ends of each touching one end of the others, I have drawn what we call a triangle. If my friend in Australia draws three straight lines on a piece of paper with both ends of each touching one end of the others, he will have drawn a triangle, too. And if I imagine three straight lines being drawn on the far side of the universe so that their ends touch, I know that this will form a triangle, too. Geometric and mathematical concepts don't apply only at a particular point in space and time; they apply throughout the universe and throughout time. These and other pure concepts inform existence but do not require it.

If I pick up the phone and talk to my friend in Australia, we will be able to quickly determine that we have both drawn a triangle. We will have little room for a difference of perception or interpretation. On the other hand, if we discuss some moral dilemma, we will each approach it from a very personal perspective, informed by experience and navigating to our individual moral compasses.

When we agree on the concept of a triangle, we work from a very direct, easily recognizable, and easily measurable set of concepts. A triangle is a closed, three-sided, straight-edged figure in a two-dimensional plane. We can leave no room for debate about the triangularity of a particular drawing.

Although any moral discussion can be fraught with disagreement, if we have defined *goodness* as that which contributes to persistence (through the persistence of existence generally: life as a form of existence, types of living organisms, and individual organisms), we can make considerable headway on any given moral question. We will only come unstuck when we disagree about whether and how a particular choice or action contributes more to persistence than another choice or action.

Similarly, in discussing morality with a living organism on another planet at the far side of the universe, we can discuss moral questions from the same ground of understanding, even if our modes of existence differ. Again, if we were to come unstuck in the course of this conversation, it would be over a difference of perspective on the particulars rather than an inability to grasp and agree on the pure basis for determining goodness.

Once we accept that the degree of goodness corresponds to the extent to which an act or action contributes to the persistence of life as a form, we must agree that morality can't be understood solely and simply through a particular religious text or teaching, or through human law. Nor can we dismiss morality as a human fiction, as a way of thinking that people have imposed on existence. Morality operates as a very pertinent and important concept, and one that, as conscious beings, we must consider in the context of the choices we make in the world.

Because the contribution of persistence to continued existence can be regarded from several perspectives—the persistence of the individual, the species, life as a form, and inanimate matter—objective morality requires us to consider what effect an act or choice will have on persistence from each of these different perspectives. Something that contributes to persistence at one level may not contribute to persistence at another.

In practical terms, our moral choices typically pertain to the persistence of living organisms and, most often, to human life. For the most part, our moral analyses focus on the three aspects of persistence of living things—life as a form, the species or group, and the individual. As we concluded earlier, choices that tend to contribute to the persistence of life as a form carry a greater moral imperative than choices that tend to contribute to the persistence of a particular species. And choices tending to contribute to the persistence of the species carry a greater moral imperative than those that tend to contribute to the persistence of a particular individual. We cannot isolate the impact of an individual act or choice on our individual persistence from the broader impact it may have on society or life in general.

The most difficult moral questions challenge us to consider and weigh the good of the individual, the species, and even other species. When judging the moral ground for medical experimentation on animals, for instance, we have to weigh the immediate harm caused to particular individuals of one species for the sake of the indirect contribution to the well-being of individuals of our own species. This kind of question prompts us to consider what best serves the persistence of life in general: the choice between sparing the animals being experimented on and saving the lives of human beings who will benefit from the anticipated medical advance, for example. But how do we judge the value of one species over another? And how do we balance the relative value of the experimentation against the cost? Such questions cannot be easily approached and may defy full analysis. When faced with such difficult moral problems, if we begin with a pure definition of morality—grounding good and bad, right and wrong, in the contribution to the persistence of life as a form—we will have an objective framework within which to work, and we can minimize the distraction and harm caused by dogmatism or ungrounded moral analysis.

To answer any moral question pertaining to living organisms, we must ultimately determine whether the act or choice will tend to make a positive contribution to the persistence of life as a form. Arriving at such a broad judgment can be made easier by first considering the impact on the particular individuals and the group or species. Typically, the effect on the individual is most readily apparent and easiest to judge. If we start with the individual and work our way out, we end up at the point of broadest and most generally applicable consideration.

Using a simple example, we can demonstrate how this process of analysis works.

If I unexpectedly become unemployed, I may be tempted to

embellish my résumé to boost my chances of landing a new job. From an individual perspective, stretching the truth has a positive impact on my persistence, if it helps me secure a position. But from a group or community perspective, my deception means that a better qualified person is denied the job, negatively affecting that person's persistence. And, with a poorly qualified person in its ranks, the company that employed me is less likely to prosper, making some portion of society less likely to persist. Most important, by lying on my résumé, I reduce (however slightly) the overall level of trust and honesty in society and the human species as a whole, harming its persistence, too.

Similarly, if we think again about the morality of medical experimentation on animals, the likely positive contribution to the persistence of those who benefit from the anticipated medical advances and the likely positive contribution to the persistence of humankind as a species, lead us to judge that medical experimentation on animals is morally right. Once we broaden our perspective to consider the overall impact on life as a form, however, we must consider the impact on the persistence of the individual animals, the animal species, and the overall impact on life, regardless of species. Only after we have thought through the ramifications for all species can we be sure that we have not made a blinkered moral judgment.

These examples, I hope, have demonstrated in a small way the objective moral process and the complexities and the difficulties of that process. For completeness, we should return briefly to the idea—which might seem strange at first—that the continued persistence of inanimate matter also carries a moral imperative. We cannot have life without matter, which preceded life as a form of existence. We cannot make choices that work against the persistence of inanimate matter in general or against particular types of inanimate matter. But we can make choices that negatively affect the persistence of a particular instance of an inanimate object—the destruction of a mountain range, for instance. In the absence of any moderating need, such choices are morally wrong.

General Illustrations of the Application of Objective Morality

Every day, each of us considers moral choices—some small and relatively insignificant, others far reaching. We arrive at moral judgments through very personal processes of reflection. Others also judge our choices, but our own judgment is and must remain all-important. Although this book points to a pure and absolute ground for moral analysis, and although in many cases we will find broad agreement on how this ground applies in general and in the particular, each moral choice compels us to analyze and understand how to apply the ground; it remains a matter of perspective and personal judgment. We can codify the process of moral analysis by working from a pure conceptual ground, but we can't assert the outcome. I therefore hesitate to provide illustrations and examples because inevitably, these illustrations will be misconstrued as statements of moral certainties. Without such illustrations and examples, however, I risk the reader's confusion about the ground and the approach to applying it.

I will therefore have to make do with a disclaimer: I cannot and do not claim to adequately or appropriately determine the morality or otherwise of any choice, either general or particular. Wiser men and women than I can provide more profound and thoughtful perspectives on the analysis of particular moral questions. I aim simply to illustrate a consistent moral framework, and to sketch out how this informs communal and personal debate on and understanding of moral questions. My views on any particular moral issue are no more complete or valid than those of anyone else.

I have done my best to keep the illustrations and examples brief and high-level, reinforcing the idea that I'm aiming at a schematic for the discussion, rather than a definitive determination. I have tried to be evenhanded, or at least to not let personal feelings override dispassion. If I have failed in this, I hope and trust that you will look past the failure and that you will not be distracted by it.

Self-Indulgence or Deprivation versus Moderation

We are each an instance of the living form. Life, as we have shown, continues to persist because its incarnations tend to persist, and because those incarnations pass on persistent traits from one generation to the next (with the nonpersistent traits tending to die out). Life would be nothing without the specific instance of the living organism—the individual. And the living organism persists, ultimately, to serve the persistence of life as a form of existence. As a particular individual, then, each of us bears the immediate responsibility for ensuring our own persistence. This constitutes a fundamental and immediate moral imperative.

We have the responsibility of caring for ourselves, feeding ourselves, avoiding unnecessary danger, growing. But as human beings we can distort these concepts and project other desires and needs through them—we can pamper ourselves, overeat, shy away from difficult situations, be lazy. Whereas spending an extra half hour in bed or spooning sugar into a cup of coffee is hardly morally wrong—such small indulgences can be restful or motivating and can contribute to persistence—extreme self-indulgence can result in health problems, underachievement, and premature aging. In other words, it can have a negative effect on persistence. Self-indulgence also tends to have a negative effect on relationships and to reduce the individual effectiveness of members of society; it has a negative effect on the persistence of the species. (Harmful extremes of self-indulgence include unrestrained hedonism, gluttony, promiscuity, sloth, cowardice, laziness, and dissolution.)

Self-deprivation represents the opposite extreme. Depriving ourselves to the extent that we jeopardize our health and well-being has a negative effect on our persistence, and extreme self-deprivation is considered wrong; suicide is an extreme example of self-deprivation.

(The ascetic uses self-deprivation as a mechanism for attaining insight and growth. Buddhist monks practice self-denial as a path to enlightenment. Can we consider these actions morally wrong? The ascetic or Buddhist impulse to self-denial rests on the premise that the material world is fleeting and illusory, and that a true and full understanding of being can only be attained by forgoing the physical being. The impulse therefore aims to transcend the physicality and the morality of the material world, an idea we'll return to later.)

Moderation presents the moral alternative to extreme self-indulgence or deprivation. The moderate individual takes care of personal needs without overindulgence or rigid self-denial. Practicing moderation, courage, prudence, temperance, and so on contribute to our persistence and are therefore judged morally good.

Egotism versus Self-Awareness

Imagine a classroom of young children, maybe six or seven years old, sitting in a circle as their teacher reads from a book. Occasionally, the teacher turns the book around, shows the children a picture, and asks a question. Invariably, a dozen little arms shoot up, dancing around, each desperate for its owner to be selected to answer. Now imagine a room full of adults attending some kind of seminar or training class. The lecturer pauses every now and then and puts forth a question. After an uncomfortable silence, one or two hands go up cautiously, tentatively, and a sense of relief washes over the room.

What happens to us as we get older? Do we lose that eagerness to chosen to give the answer? Do we just suppress it?

Just as the concept of self appears as the first and most fundamental aspect of consciousness, the concept of other appears immediately and directly as its necessary opposite. From this point forward we spend our lives assessing our sense of self, comparing ourselves to others, and forming concepts about our place in the world, the way others see us. The infant who realizes that she has a self and that this means others have selves, too, has started on the lifelong quest for balance between being self-centric and selfless. As an adult, in her sanest moments, she will understand that others' egos press and cajole as much as hers, that everyone is struggling against the impression that the world revolves around him or her. At times, we all skew the balanced perspective of self versus other through fear and loneliness, through a desire to be noticed and loved.

Those first-graders with a frantic desire to be chosen to answer have a more direct connection to the egotistical pleasure of pride than the adults in the lecture hall. But the adults in the lecture hall have a much more developed awareness of the futility of pride, the pleasure and appropriateness of modesty.

* * * * *

Impulses or feelings that cause us to inflate our own needs, desires, and self-images at the expense of others sometimes contribute to individual persistence by improving our chances to further goals and ambitions, but we will, ultimately, tend to harm our persistence if we are egotistic. And even successful egotists, generally speaking, do poorly in social relationships and damage the persistence of the groups or communities to which they belong. Society tends to work more effectively and to prosper when each member maintains a fairly balanced and sensitive perspective of himself in relation to fellow citizens. So we feel instinctively that selfishness, pride, envy, narcissism (vanity), and greed are negative qualities. Self-awareness provides a more objective view of our needs and desires in comparison with the needs and desires of others; it allows us to overcome the press of our pride and desire for recognition.

Oppression versus Selflessness

The infant who recognizes her self as distinct from others has taken her first step into consciousness. The child or adult who perceives that there is no difference between her self and the self of others and that, as living organisms, we are each a representative of the form of life—the tsetse fly as much as the pope—has recognized the fundamental morality of persistence in the form of life itself. Every choice we make that might affect the persistence of other living organisms incurs a moral responsibility. Just as we bear an immediate responsibility to look to our own persistence, we bear a responsibility to look to the persistence of others.

Whereas self-indulgence and egotism can affect others indirectly, any choice that aims to satisfy our own ends at the expense of others tends to have a very direct negative effect on the persistence of other individuals and the broader community. The rationale presents itself too clearly to require explanation. Obvious examples include exploitation, bigotry, nepotism, faithlessness, cruelty, neglect, torture, and cold-blooded murder.

Although cold-blooded murder clearly belongs in this category, the general concept of killing presents a more complicated analysis. Taking another person's life in defense of one's own life or the life of another, for instance, tends to contribute generally to persistence. And living organisms kill and are killed every day for food. Similarly, we can see that deceit tends to work against the persistence of human society unless the deceiver deceives to prevent some greater harm.

In contrast, impulses to balance our needs with the needs of others, and to put the needs of others before our own, we term generally as selflessness. Through selflessness, we tend to contribute to the persistence of other individuals and to the persistence of society as a whole. Selflessness is therefore judged to be good. Examples of selflessness include love, kindness, generosity, charity, public service, and heroism.

War versus Peace

Every conflict between two groups involves a clash of concepts. From the broadest perspective, the form of life cares only for its persistence and favors no particular organism over another. In human society, no race, culture, religious group, country, or community has any stronghold on the right to persist. We're all instances of the form of life, and we're all here to serve the persistence of the form of life. When we fight over ideological differences, or to protect property or sovereignty, we fight over the concept that one community's ideology, right to property, or right to self-rule supersedes another's. But it is clear that war works against the persistence of the individuals of both communities, as well as the persistence of the communities themselves. War generally tends to work against the persistence of individuals, communities, and societies; it can thus be judged on this basis to be generally wrong.

Under certain circumstances, the avoidance of war or capitulation to the demands or rule of another power leads to a far greater threat to the persistence of individuals and society. In these situations, active resistance is the most morally viable choice (for instance, the war against Nazi Germany or, more recently, the wars in what was once Yugoslavia, and the call for intervention in the African genocides). On this basis, we judge it morally right to resist and fight regimes that work against the persistence of entire communities and peoples. Diplomatic, respectful, and peaceful coexistence between societies tends to contribute to the persistence of the human species and is therefore judged to be morally good.

Conservatism versus Liberalism

Conservatism and liberalism, its counterpart, derive from fundamental, universal concepts—all societies at all times have encompassed some variations of these two perspectives, which have in turn defined and divided two general modes of thinking. Conservatism tends to emphasize the importance of norms and traditions; it can be defined by its reaction against differences from the norm. It also tends to emphasize the rights and responsibilities of the individual to protect and perpetuate these norms, more than the rights and responsibilities of the central government. Liberalism, on the other hand, encourages openness to variety within the community and embraces change; it places faith in the benefit of organized and centralized social infrastructure to help balance the inevitable inequities that exist in any large group.

In the United States today, for example, conservatives prefer to let the market prevail and to minimize the role of central government; they work to confirm and strengthen traditional (faith-based and family) values while resisting the influence of "nontraditional" ways of life. Conservatism aims to empower the individual to account for her own place in the market and in society. Conservative government typically intervenes reactively rather than proactively in asserting and reinforcing these goals. In conservatism, government champions the right of the individual to make the correct choices, until she proves incapable of doing so.

Conservatives approve of the status quo and seek to maintain a traditional mode of human society. They have a static viewpoint, which leads to a protectionist perspective. Conservatives resist change and emphasize the rightness of the norm, or standard. Conservatism protects and elevates the importance of the individual who embodies or reflects this norm (an extreme example being the tendency of conservatives to want to preserve the culture and racial identity of the majority at the expense of the minority). So long as individual choices don't work against the persistence of society, conservatives emphasize the importance of individual persistence.

On issues of morality and values, the conservative reacts against the different, a response that emerges from a fear of the unknown and unfamiliar. Homosexuality, for example, seems to threaten to the institution of family. The conservative fears that it could lead to a general disintegration of the family structure. To the moral conservative, even the thought and concept of homosexuality can be repugnant, a threat to his own type and to the persistence of the way of life he feels is right. (What greater threat to the persistence of a family-based society than the idea that the family structure itself will fall apart?)

Conservatism does not embrace the concept that the persistence of life as a form carries the greatest moral imperative, and that this imperative must trump the importance of the persistence of a particular society in order for life to persist. It implicitly rejects the perspective that a society or species can and must evolve and change. Conservatives hold a blinkered and truncated perspective on the moral spectrum, and conservative thinking can and does conflict with the overriding moral imperative of the persistence of life as a form. (This helps to explain why the fundamentalist religious right in America supports the idea that the world was created intact, that human beings did not evolve, that a divine creator put us on earth in his likeness. This extreme perspective shelters the conservative from the possibility that the way of living which feels right and proper to him is naturally subject to change and has no greater claim on legitimacy than what came before or what might yet come.)

Economic conservatism starts from an impulse to keep economic decisions as close to the individual and family unit as possible. The individual and the local community know best how to control their own finances. Conservatives don't like the idea of having the government make decisions about the general good. The conservative makes her own way and chooses her own charity. The conservative places faith in and pays more attention to the local community than to society generally. From a governmental perspective, the conservative wants to be assured that society generally shares similar values (the conservative family wants its government to help ensure that other communities operate in the same way). Therefore, as with moral conservatism, economic conservatism works to support the persistence of the individual and the social group that helps itself while remaining suspicious of or reacting against attempts to pool economic and political resources for the betterment of the broader society. Again, this approach tends to limit government's involvement in furthering the persistence of life as a form.

On this basis, to the extent that it can and does work against the persistence of life as a form, conservatism would be judged wrong. To emphasize the qualification, conservatism can be judged wrong only inasmuch as the conservative perspective works against the persistence of life as a form by supporting the persistence of a particular way of life or society. Examples of conservatism generally judged to be wrong include the conservative reactions against the abolition of slavery, segregation, racially mixed marriage, homosexual marriage, unrestricted imports, and foreign culture.

Conservatism can be defined as a mode of thinking and interacting that reflects a basic desire of the living entity to persist in its current form and to encourage persistence of its current form. In the context of the individual and of the species, conservatism can be right and good. But when set against that which leads to the persistence of life as a form, unadulterated conservatism can result in modes of thinking and choices and behaviors that restrict persistence and are therefore wrong.

Liberalism, on the other hand, incorporates the idea that the persistence of life as a form carries the highest moral imperative—that the importance of the individual and society must remain subordinate to this primary imperative. Liberals tend to support federal programs that aim to level the economic playing field or provide safety nets rather than allowing market forces to provide economic balance. This robs the individual and the local community of the full right and will to choose their own way in the economic world. The liberal aims to strike a balance between individual freedom and the good of all. From a moral perspective, liberals support the choice of the individual—even when it deviates from the norm—and tend to defend change, even those influences that irretrievably alter the societal norm.

Economic liberalism tends to suppress the fullest economic will of the individual, and to work against the creative life force by moving toward a leveling out of the economic playing field (that is, seeking that field's lowest common denominator). Thus, liberalism tends to operate against the persistence of certain individuals in favor of humanity generally, and in some cases it works against the persistence of a particular society. The liberal impulse aims to remove arbitrary inequality and injustice, and to remove the worst (and avoidable) ravages of poverty, disease, and oppression wherever and why ever they exist. Liberalism, when granted this urge, wills the persistence of most individuals (particularly the disadvantaged), the social group (by making the whole stronger), and life as a form (through embracing change and seeking to move the whole forward).

Moral liberalism is often attacked as a degenerative and destructive mode of thinking and choosing. It embraces ideas and choices that work against the persistence of the traditional family group and that can lead to destabilizing change in the structure of society generally. But the liberal impulse encourages change and thereby supports the possibility of adaptation.

Liberalism generally and generically has been associated with ideas and choices that threaten the established mold and shake things up so that progress can be made. Therefore, in its conceptual form, liberalism is the conscious and temperamental embodiment of the will to persist in the form of life.

Particular Illustrations of the Application of Objective Morality

Today, pitting armed warriors against one another as a form of sport and spectacle is considered morally repulsive; it's also illegal. Two thousand years ago, the people of ancient Rome flocked in their thousands to see gladiators fight to the death. Emperors promoted gladiatorial contests as a form of release and entertainment for the citizens, and the people loved them. Although grounded in an absolute, our moral judgment reflects our relative assessment of the circumstances and particulars, and it changes according to our perception of those circumstances and particulars.

For the purposes of illustration, the previous section explored some general moral concepts, demonstrating how one might apply an overall assessment of rightness or wrongness through the degree of contribution of a choice or action to persistence. I attempted to stay with general illustrations and to keep them at arm's length, to emphasize the concepts. Although such illustrations will, I hope, help to show how we can use an objective moral framework based on persistence to inform and guide abstract moral inquiry, they don't work so well in demonstrating how we address the kinds of real, complex, personal moral questions and choices we face every day.

We cannot elaborate all of the moral choices that occur in real life. Each person faces an enormous and far-reaching range of moral choices. But this need not daunt someone who is trying to bring to his or her own life an objective basis for understanding problems and dilemmas and the choices that spring from them. If we can address a particular moral issue by focusing on why certain choices are good or bad, we can illuminate our confusion with a more rational perspective.

Of course, such a process should not be used mechanically, without considering our feelings and instincts, which provide direct and pertinent information about our moral sensitivity. Feelings and instincts can sometimes mislead us, but only if we don't fully acknowledge and understand them. If we feel that a particular choice is wrong, no matter how much we think we've proved to ourselves logically and objectively that it is right, then we have a mismatch between objective reasoning and feeling. We should seek to resolve this conflict through further reflection and soul searching, by digging into the feeling of wrongness and understanding its basis. The process I'm describing is intended to remove or reduce the influence of prejudice, to expand a narrow perspective, to enlighten selfish or narrow motives. It is not intended to provide a systematic, foolproof formula to follow when making life choices.

Second, two individuals faced with the same objective set of circumstances may not draw the same moral conclusions. Each person necessarily holds a unique perspective and must arrive at his or her own moral choices. But by seeking to apply an objective moral framework based on persistence, we can hope to reveal the source of differences and disagreements so that they can be resolved.

Last, communication, discussion, and dialogue can be enormously valuable, though they are not strictly necessary when making a life choice or arriving at a moral judgment. Communication should always aim to establish an open, honest, and generous perspective. We don't want to seek the counsel of those we can't trust, but the objective opinion of those we can trust helps to unfog our judgment, showing how we're aligning our thinking too closely with our own perspective.

Again, I cannot stress too strongly that I aim only to illustrate the process, not to draw conclusions about the wrong or right of particular moral dilemmas. Moral policy should be debated by those with profound and proven insight and sensitivity (that is, not me), and founded on their wisdom. Each of us must make our own moral choices, however, guided and influenced by our own experience, by the counsel of those we trust, and through reaching peace with our feelings, instincts, and objective perspectives. I hope that the framework for an objective morality grounded in the principle of persistence can enlighten and support us in making our choices; this much we can ask of it, and no more.

I Have Eaten the Plums...

William Carlos Williams's (1934) poem "This Is Just to Say" is written in the form of a personal note, an apology from the protagonist to someone he lives with. The writer of the note, arriving home late, has eaten the plums that had been carefully set aside in the icebox, presumably to eat for breakfast.

Williams's note writer lovingly evokes the joy and guilt of eating the deliciously cool, sweet plums. When making the choice to eat the plums, he was aware, it seems, that he would disappoint or even anger the plums' owner by choosing to satisfy rather than forgo his own desire and appetite. By apologizing, he shows that even though he judged it morally preferable to deny the self, he chose another path. His sense of morality did not deflect his course, but it did affect his thoughts and feelings and, we imagine, the thoughts and feelings of the plums' owner, as well.

At a primary and fundamental level, the plum eater acts in support of his individual persistence—he takes in sustenance, answering his basic needs and desires as an organism. Expanding our perspective to include the other individual, the plum eater works against the persistence of the plums' owner by depriving him or her of sustenance. From the perspective of individual persistence, the act is neutral—one individual organism gains, another loses. Life as a form of existence is even. (This simple equation describes much of the world of animal behavior—this is survival of the fittest.)

Broadening our perspective further, we can consider the impact on the social bonds between the two protagonists. Generally, when two people form a social partnership, it provides an advantage to the persistence of both. When one is in need, the other can come to her aid. Working together, two people can also accomplish things that one person cannot accomplish alone. A partnership is the narrowest example of a community or social group. That which contributes to the persistence of the social group will contribute to the persistence of life as a form. The greater the degree of trust and cooperation, the more successful the partnership. By eating the plums, the note writer undermines this trust and cooperation (he acknowledges this directly by saying, "Forgive me"). So, even though from the perspective of individual persistence his choice is neutral, from the perspective of the persistence of the social group (this partnership) his choice is morally wrong.

Now, what if Williams's protagonist had opened the icebox,

seen the plums, and eaten them without even considering the possibility that the other person had put them there to eat for breakfast? He would have had no awareness of depriving their owner of breakfast, no knowing betrayal, no poem, no apology. Would this change the morality of the act, and if so, how?

From the plum eater's perspective, in this altered circumstance, his choice is good: he has acted in accordance with his needs and desires, and, as far as he knows, his actions have had no adverse effect on persistence generally. But if we presume that the other person will be disappointed or hurt (by taking the trouble to set the plums aside, only to have someone else eat them), then from an objective perspective, the note writer has acted wrongly. Whether he knows it or not, his choice has had a negative impact on the trust and cooperation between him and the plums' owner. Whether he knows it or not, he has contributed less to the persistence of life as a form than if he had thought about and been sensitive to the impact of his actions on the other person and their relationship (partnership).

In apologizing, the note writer reveals that he is aware of his wrong, and in writing the poem he aims to mitigate that wrong. He has wrapped up his lapse in words that evoke the plums, their tempting coolness and sweetness, his weakness, his sensitivity to the other's feelings. He leaves the gift of a poem in place of the plums, hoping it will perhaps fully restore or even strengthen the bonds between him and the plums' owner. He may have decided to write the apology before taking the plums. The whole event may be an elaborate game, demonstrating and confessing his selfishness while highlighting his generosity and sensitivity. I took your plums, yes, he may be saying, but I left you something more personal and valuable in their place.

(What makes Williams's poem a poem, what makes it interesting as a poem, is Williams's playful but sensitive sketch of the moral concepts—his portrayal of his willful transgression, his weakness, his flouting of his own moral principles. He has done what we all feel drawn to do from time to time: to choose the moral wrong, to give in to our selfish will. The open confession of even such a minor transgression, one perhaps easily forgiven, evokes awe, and in our awe we are forced to recognize in his weakness our own.)

Wild Plums

Grace Stone Coates's (1929) "Wild Plums" tells the story of a young child of proud, poor parents. Her father wants to set himself apart from his neighbors: he keeps his plow in a shed rather than leaving it out in the elements. He disdains the cart trips that his neighbors take to collect wild plums. The girl's mother feels ambivalent, torn between a desire to respect her husband and his choices and a yearning for greater freedom. She seems to long for a closer connection to her sensual will. If not for him, we think, she would go with the others to pick the wild plums. The child, being a child, longs for the adventure of going with her neighbors on the wagon and doesn't see any harm in it.

To some extent then the child's mother agrees with her husband that it can sometimes be preferable to suppress one's immediate instincts and desires. The father puts his plows in a shed not only to keep them safe from the elements, but also to show that he is orderly and has the self-discipline to put his tools away rather than take the easy route and leave them where they stand. Self-discipline tends to lead to the persistence of the individual and, when exercised appropriately, tends to lead to the persistence of society and the species.

But the father's pride in his self-discipline tends to undermine his ability to form social bonds and, in that way, works against the persistence of the social group—his neighbors tolerate him, but the bonds of neighborliness and friendship could be deeper if he were not so proud. The mother senses this, and understanding their feelings as well as his creates a tension that forms the core of her dilemma. Does she side with her husband in order to preserve and keep strong the bond she has with him (persistence of the immediate family group), or does she stand up to the prideful aspects of his self-discipline and make choices that reflect her own sense of what is appropriate?

She wants to go with the neighbors to pick wild plums and to take her daughter with her, but she wants to do so with her husband's blessing. She argues her case with her husband. He is resolute. She ultimately decides to side with her husband. Not only does she decline the offer to go with the neighbors to pick the wild fruit, but she also refuses to let her daughter go.

Her decision has implications on various levels. The first is that she has opted to reinforce (by not standing strong against) the prideful aspect of her husband's desire for self-discipline. She wants to maintain the marriage bond, but ultimately her weakness erodes their relationship; she has sided with him despite herself, and she resents him for forcing her to such choices. She wants to avoid the husband's disapproval, even though she believes that such disapproval is morally wrong (because it tends to work against the persistence of society as a whole). She has not accepted his perspective—she has submitted to it.

She has also implicated her daughter in her weakness. When asked, the girl says she would go with the neighbors. The mother then forbids her daughter to even accept a gift of wild plums. (She has worked against the persistence of future generations by providing an example of moral weakness.)

Famous Blue Raincoat

Leonard Cohen wrote the song "Famous Blue Raincoat" (1970) in the form of a letter to a friend. In it, Cohen reveals that his friend once had an affair with Jane, Cohen's wife. The song seems to indicate, on one hand, that Cohen feels betrayed by his friend and, on the other, Cohen's recognition that the affair had been a good thing for Jane, that it helped her to grow in some way or to shed some sadness. The song bleeds with the poignancy of this dual perspective.

Nothing in the song indicates that Cohen's friend thought through the moral consequences of his actions. On the contrary, small and subtle clues reveal a narcissistic character, particularly the use of the word *famous* to describe his raincoat. Cohen, on the other hand, has thought through the moral consequences to both himself and Jane. He has determined that the affair helped Jane, and he sees his own error in too easily giving up on the possibility of helping her grow. Through reflection, he has worked to put aside his own feelings of betrayal and jealousy and has grudgingly forgiven his friend's betrayal.

Cohen has considered what course of action will tend to lead to the persistence of his partnership with Jane, his friendship with the man he is writing to, and the improved persistence (through her personal growth) of Jane as an individual. He has set against these considerations his individual perspective and the immediate demands of his ego and has judged them less important.

Beyond Morality

It has begun to snow. The flakes cast about on the hard edges of the air as if self-willed, making their way down with heady stealth. The night holds me in its cloister, whispered secrets circling its cold stone walls. I am one with the bitter fingers of cold, with the empty blackness. My thoughts shimmer and dance with the lights from stores and streetlights and cars. Doubt has been folded back, pressed out, like the daylight. I am neither unconscious nor conscious of knowing. My legs and feet move with the sidewalk, turning the earth beneath me. I am one soul alone; I am the universe.

What is right, what is wrong? The pressing questions of morality have fled, do not exist, or perhaps are existence itself. Gloveless, scarfless, hatless. The snow lands and perishes on my skin, each flake a new moment, a new me. There is nothing to decide, nothing to be thought through. Instead, existence acts through me, uses me as a conduit. I neither pass through the night, nor enter it. I am the night. The night is me. I am not myself, yet never more myself.

The brilliant crystals cosset me in white weightless powder. I feel myself rising up and out, a torrent. I laugh and spin, face upward toward the twirling gray mass. This moment will last forever, forever alive, forever sure. This brief walk is eternity, is me, is truth, is everything and nothing.

I take out my keys, free the latch from its stay, push the door, enter the house, leaving the vastness behind me. The warm house air stirs eddying currents of knowledge and reason. I brush at the dead white flakes and they spill away from my hand, falling in clumps to the floor. My fingers turn each button out of its hole. I open my coat and a rush of warmth rises from my body, surprising me.

* * * * *

There is that which we do and there is that which we think and feel: for each of us, two realms—the outer and the inner. The border of these realms is in the decisions we make—to act or not to act, what we will do, what we won't do. This is the territory of morality, the process of deciding whether doing something or not doing something is good or bad. The moral conscience is the border guard between the perceptual and the real. There is no morality without conscious choice, without reflection. Everything else is instinct, raw being.

As conscious beings we can grasp and understand conceptual objects outside the concepts that represent material existence. We can conceive of things that don't exist and could never exist. We can therefore appreciate that material existence is not a necessary condition, and neither does it encompass all conceivable possibilities.

And we can accept that our existence, and the totality of material existence, is transitory and conditional. Once we accept this, we must agree that the meaning of existence is similarly constrained and finite. We came from nothing and we will return to nothing. What happens in between has meaning and importance only to the extent that we grant it such meaning and importance.

Those who reject the importance of existence, of our part in existence, of the goodness of contributing to rather than working against persistence, cannot simply be labeled irrational; such a perspective can be completely rational. The person who understands that her existence has positive meaning only with respect to the continued existence of the universe we live in, and that this universe will eventually, in all likelihood, cease to exist, may be tempted to give up on life and retreat from the instincts that instruct us to care for ourselves and others. This helps to explain two extreme modes of rejection—the path to enlightenment (letting go of self and the material world) taken by various spiritual devotees and the anarchy, hedonism, and amorality of existentialism.

Given that morality—good and bad, right and wrong—functions through and for existence, both of these perspectives are morally wrong. The religious devotee seeks to absent himself from the rigors and responsibilities of persistence. He tends to harm his own material persistence and the persistence of others by refuting the importance of material existence and making choices consistent with that perspective. The existential hedonist or immoralist works indirectly and often directly against her own persistence and the persistence of others. If we consider a perspective not limited to our mode of existence, we cannot reject as irrational the choice of seeking enlightenment or of living amorally; these choices are wrong only in the context of material existence.

Why, then, act morally? What can we say to the person who chooses to reject morality? With what sense of meaning and purpose can we inspire ourselves and our children to care about our moral choices?

The answer is simple, clear, and completely pragmatic: I do exist, I am alive. I can either choose to act against my mode of being, or in accordance with it. I do not have another mode of being, nor will I ever have one. I have this one life, and to the extent that I embrace and act in accordance with my mode of being, I am more likely to suffer less and feel greater contentment and value.

We cannot criticize the Buddhist monk for seeking enlightenment through complete release of the ego—by letting go of the need to satisfy its demands, but we can say that he will not achieve more through such a search—his search will show that there is nothing more to achieve than an awareness that existence is futile and ultimately meaningless. He could start at this point, however, and still find meaning within life, within each choice, through acting in accordance with his mode of being rather than absenting himself from it.

Every conscious being must accept that the scope of individual existence is bounded by the concept of persistence. We can choose to contribute to this persistence or not. We will be faced with these choices every day, and they will sometimes present us with enormous and seemingly insuperable challenges that we can avoid or face. If we choose to face them we contribute to something that is not absolute, not given, not infinite or immortal, but from which we have been born and to which our contribution can bring limited, finite, temporary but real meaning.

Section 4: Understanding Our Lives

It's curious that we don't give more thought to our existence, to the meaning of our lives, to the reasons we live as we do. Most of us get up each morning, experience and work through the joys and challenges of the day, and go to bed at night without once thinking about the bigger context of our thoughts, feelings, and actions. The persistent and immediate demands on our time and attention naturally limit our perspective. Although we are conscious and cerebral beings, we must live in the moment in order to survive and to derive satisfaction from our existence. Who has time to think about the bigger picture?

But we do, from time to time. And all of us at one time or another—because of a particular life experience or a certain set of circumstances, or simply when enjoying a few moments of quiet thought—have wondered what it all means and how it all fits together, why we're here and why our lives are as they are.

We can use an objective morality to help us understand the right and wrong of particular choices in particular circumstances; we can also consider how our lives generally embody and reflect the principles of existence. Life has persisted as a form because the form of life sustains itself. Human beings possess particular characteristics and traits that have developed according to the principle of persistence. By looking at our lives from this perspective, we can understand more about why we exist as we do.

Life's Span and Arc

Two years ago, my father died of cancer. He was in his mid-sixties, not an old man by today's standards. It seemed unfair that he should die then, only a couple of years after retirement. He was an active person, always avidly involved in some pursuit that typically had a physical component—running, climbing, building things. If he hadn't fallen ill, he would have remained active for years to come.

Why do we have the life spans that we do? Why do we have a sense of a short life or a long life? How do we understand the ravages of disease, the tragedy of accidents?

As a species, we live as long as we should in order for life to persist. Different species have very different life spans. Some creatures live for just a few days. Some trees live for many hundreds of years. Under normal circumstances, the average life span of members of a particular species will be appropriate to the persistence of that variety of the life form. In other words, things tend to live as long as they need to or can without jeopardizing the existence of their type.

The fruit fly's short life span enables it to move rapidly through generations, giving it the ability to adapt to new conditions and to multiply at an incredible pace when conditions support a large community. Insect populations tend to wax and wane abruptly between wide extremes. This favors the persistence of the insect archetype, which otherwise is vulnerable to conditions that might threaten its persistence. Redwoods, on the other hand, take their time to grow; the redwood form has no particular need to adapt quickly. Redwoods plod on and up year in, year out. Their structure lends itself to slow steady growth and gradual population shifts. Redwoods are in it for the long haul.

Some animals live longer than humans (turtles and tortoises can live well over a hundred years, as can some fish), but as an animal species, we enjoy a relatively long life span. And we are living much longer than most of our ancestors. With improvements in the general quality of life, sanitation, protection against and eradication of diseases, the average human life span has increased dramatically over the past two thousand years, and most dramatically over the past two hundred years. At the time of the Roman empire, a person could expect to live to be about twenty-eight years old. By the end of the eighteenth century, the average age at death had increased to about thirty-seven, and now human life expectancy is up to more than seventy years.

If we relate the human life span and its stages to the persistence of the human species, we see how the arc of our lives contributes to our persistence: human beings have a relatively long period of infancy, childhood, and adolescence. Our brains and bodies don't stop growing until we reach about age seventeen or eighteen. This long growth period allows us to develop our sophisticated mental capabilities. As a species, we have adapted to cope with infants who need constant nurturing and protection over an extended period. Even after infancy, children need our protection and tutoring over many more years before they can operate effectively and independently in the world. For the human species, the development of a sophisticated mental awareness—of consciousness, language, higher reasoning—has enabled us to persist more effectively. We have used these skills to survive in otherwise harsh conditions, to find new food sources and shelter from the elements, to protect ourselves against predators, and to develop complex interdependent communities.

Upon maturation, women have about twenty years in which to bear and begin to raise children. Today, a woman who gives birth in her early forties can expect to remain physically fit and capable while her child grows to maturity. Residents of more developed countries tend to marry and have children later than was customary in the past. The longer life expectancy and generally higher quality of life in developed countries allows couples and individuals the freedom to delay starting their families without fear that they will be absent or incapacitated before their children reach maturity.

Children reach adolescence at an age when, today, we consider them too young to cope with the demands of parenting. This may seem anomalous, but adaptation works through time and numbers. Over time, human sexual development may move closer to the stage at which young adults have achieved full physical and mental maturation. At present, the strong social influence of family and society works to prevent children from having children.

(Because family and society typically step in to help care for children born to adolescents or very young adults, however, any inherited trend toward later sexual maturation may be softened.)

The period of prime physical and mental maturity from our late teenage years through to (these days) our early fifties corresponds to the span of time when we contribute most to the persistence of our form of life, and life generally. We can raise families, protect, nurture, and create. In this period we use our physical and mental powers to their full. Given that the expectation of living to age fifty or more has only become reasonable in the past two hundred years, the phenomenon of a gradual physical decline through our sixties and seventies is a new one. By combating disease and extending our life span, human beings now live beyond the period of prime physical and mental productivity of the human type. As we reach sixty and seventy and beyond, our bodies and minds eventually begin to wear down and deteriorate. (My father's knees had started to fail him even before the cancer hit.)

This too will likely change. The persistence of the human form will be best served by adapting to our improved quality of life, by an evolution toward a longer period of prime physical and mental health. Our sophisticated conscious awareness and our connected ability to learn and retain knowledge and wisdom mean that it will be advantageous to the persistence of the human species for us to live longer and grow old later. Societies and communities will have longer collective memories. Wisdom and learning will be passed on more effectively and provide greater continuity and balance from one generation to the next. Most of us today know or have known one or more of our grandparents. A society with a collective memory long enough to recall and form choices based on direct life lessons learned fifty and seventy years ago (rarely possible today), is less likely to repeat history's mistakes, and more likely to assure its persistence as a species and a form of life.

The Ego

The ego (our human sense of self and the importance of self) corresponds directly to our conscious awareness of our persistence as individuals and the importance of that persistence. Without the ego, we would have no direct regard for our self-preservation or development. "I want, I need, I must have…" the ego says.

We are all familiar with the demands of the ego: the need to eat, the desire to have sex, to be safe, to be loved, to relax, to create. In most cases, the ego exaggerates its demands—when we want things, we think we need them. Those of us who live affluent lives in affluent societies do not know true need. We get hungry, but we don't know starvation.

The ego's inflated sense of importance is at once a survival mechanism and an evolutionary hangover that will subside with time. As human beings have evolved and developed, we have learned to balance the demands of the ego against the demands or needs of others or of the broader community. We form social partnerships and groups that operate with some sense of balance between the needs and desires of the individual members of the group. In emergent societies and cultures, the ego tends to dominate more strongly than it does in established societies where the rules of law and social etiquette demand respect for and tolerance of the needs of others and of society generally. It is interesting that the smaller and more intimate the social group, the greater the tension between ego and selflessness (the best example perhaps being a love relationship in which each person struggles to maintain his or her sense of self and not forgo his or her own desires, while simultaneously desiring the growth and fulfillment of the other).

Societies and social and religious movements and philosophies have strived and continue to strive to achieve the ideal balance between the egos of their members and the needs of the group. As mentioned previously, Buddhism teaches that the attainment of true enlightenment comes only through the full and complete release of the ego. The ascetic takes no food or drink, transcends pain and desire, and gradually withers away into physical nonbeing. Communism subordinates the needs of the individual to the greater good of society. Democracy seeks to let the ego find its own balance with the needs of society as a whole. Selfishness, nihilism, and oppression place the ego in a position of destructive and dangerous prominence, working against the persistence of the species and the form of life itself.

On a personal level, achieving the right balance between the demands of our egos and the needs of our community presents us with a constant, important, and testing challenge throughout our lives. We typically contribute most to persistence when we can put all but the most urgent wants of the ego to one side and focus on the needs of others. When we contribute to society generally or to the preservation of the environment, when we take on roles in the service of others without looking for personal gain, we tend to increase the chance that the human form and the form of life in general will continue to grow and persist.

Finding this balance and understanding the ego can be hard. Social etiquette leads us to suppress our awareness of and expression of certain primary demands of the ego—lust, for instance. The very word connotes an impulse that doesn't conform to polite social norms. And yet lust simply reflects the basic urge to reproduce. Where would our species be without the urge to reproduce? We need to acknowledge our lust, the necessity and goodness of this feeling, and balance it with the social acceptability of expressing it or acting on it. Similarly, anger reflects the ego's sense of actual or threatened violation. It is the urge for defense through attack. Without anger, we would be stunted in our ability to defend our persistence or the persistence of our family and community. Thus, we need to acknowledge our anger rather than suppressing or denying it. But we also need to put it into context, to balance our desire to express and act on it with our desire to moderate and redirect our feelings.

Family

When I wake up on a Saturday morning at 5:30 a.m. to my one-year-old's insistent cries, I wonder in my sleep-deprived haze why anyone would have children. Fortunately, after my first cup of coffee, the answer presents itself with the simplicity and directness of that same infant—we have children because without children the human species would cease to exist. And without family we would be poorly placed to ensure the persistence of our children. The family provides critical nurturing to infants and children. Some societies extend the idea of family quite broadly; others constrain it to include only the parents and siblings. But whatever its particular definition, a family helps to ensure that infants and children will grow to maturity.

Thus, the critical requirements and role of family are self-evident, but the more subtle concepts and importance of family are less so. In most social groups, there exists an element of choice. We can choose our friends, our colleagues. We can move from one community to another. But with family we have no choice. This applies just as well to formal or informal adoptive families. Family members rely on one another or expect to be able to rely on one another.

The family group tends to be more immediately important to us than our neighbors and members of society generally. The family becomes an extension of the ego. We feel the desires and needs of family members as more keenly akin to our own than those of nonfamily members. Protecting family comes second only to protection of self in guaranteeing the immediate persistence of our species.

And, as with the ego, our relationship to and interaction with our families and their effects on our choices call for balance. The greatest good will be served if we put the needs of society generally ahead of the less-than-critical wants of our families. Striking the right balance here, too, presents a lifelong challenge.

It is interesting to note that, although most of us recognize the tension between selfishness and selflessness on an individual level, we do not always see as clearly the tension between the needs of family and the needs of society. Even our ethics and laws waver between the two: a husband or wife can opt not to testify against his or her spouse. When faced with the prospect of turning in a family member who has committed a crime, many opt not to. As with the ego, if we can remain aware of how family bonds can bring us into conflict with the greater good of society, we will be better placed to choose the right course of action in a particular situation.

Love

To love means to value the essence of another person, and therefore his or her persistence. Through love, we rise above the self-centered demands and desires of the ego. Love, then, contributes greatly to the persistence of humankind as a species, as well as the persistence of life as a form in itself. But love, as we know, does not always seem so straightforward.

Animals without consciousness act instinctively to protect and nurture others. But the ground of love begins with the conscious awareness that the self is indistinguishable in importance from the nonself. Love is a conscious instinct, even though we experience it as a nonintellectual, nonconscious sensation. (Small children experience feelings of love, but only after separating their awareness of self from nonself.) Love as a concept represents a new level of awareness and brings with it a new set of possibilities for the persistence of life.

The rabbit that thumps the ground at the first sign of danger, or the bird that swoops and pecks to protect its nest, does so out of instinct, without conscious choice. Consciousness and conscious awareness of the value of love bring to humans the possibility of performing great service to the persistence of others and life in general. We can and do choose to make sacrifices for the good of others. The awareness of love as a concept and the conscious choice of loving action have contributed greatly to the persistence of humankind.

One difficulty with understanding love comes when we mistake or mislabel other feelings for feelings of love. Scott Peck, in *The Road Less Traveled* (1978), discusses how we use the word *love* when referring to an extension of the ego to incorporate another person or thing. I say that I love my stereo system, but what I really mean is that I have brought the concept of my stereo system and my interactions with it under the umbrella of my feelings about myself, under the canopy of my ego. I feel a surge of possessive pride and warmth when I think about my stereo. I want to protect and nurture it, preserve it, but these feelings reflect on my ego only; I associate the stereo with myself. Peck uses the term *cathexis* to distinguish this kind of feeling from the feeling of love, which is egoless.

We also often confuse or overlap feelings of real love with cathexis. We may have genuine feelings of love for another person, while at the same time cathecting the concept of that person or their qualities. And we can feel genuine love for a person at times, while at other times feeling only a connection of loyalty or familiarity. Our capacity for love and love's tension with the ego varies over time and from one set of circumstances to another. Love is not a static, reliable thing. It can seem to be so, because often love remains once we strip away our selfish or defensive feelings.

If we consider the association between feelings of love between men and women, sexual desire, and procreation, we expose another complication in our understanding of love. Sexual attraction and the resulting close connections between people also cause us to suppress our egos, to forgo to some extent the needs and desires of the self in favor of the other. Despite the obvious parallels, though, something quite different from love is at work.

Sexual attraction and desire, and the feelings that we refer to as "being in love," don't start from a separation of self from non-self, but from the opposite—a nonconscious, instinctive forgoing of self, a merging of the ego with the projection of one's ego onto the other. This process has developed as an evolutionary necessity in order for our species to reproduce. Falling in love is life's way of blinding one, temporarily, to the flaws and foibles of another person so that one sees only good attractive qualities in him or her. (This helps to explain why, when we fall out of love, often we are left without any lasting feelings of egoless love for a partner. Falling "in love" contributes to our persistence through ensuring reproduction, whereas experiencing "love" reflects an evolution toward choices that can make a broad and general contribution to the persistence of life as a form.)

We can also experience general feelings of love. Various spiritual teachings center on the idea of forgoing the ego and accepting others as they are. By putting aside our egos, we can accept and love others. This tends to serve the persistence of humankind and of life generally by leading to greater cooperation, less conflict, and more understanding and tolerance.

But what about unequivocal tolerance, total passivity, bottomless love? When some force or movement—political or social, personal or public—threatens the persistence of people or of life, we may not respond egotistically, but we should respond. If we don't try to stop tyranny and murder, we cannot further the persistence of humankind. This does not mean that we must forgo or act outside love, but that we should not regard love as a panacea. Love does not free us from difficult choices; it forces us to respond to difficult choices through awareness and acceptance of the other rather than through anger and ego.

Friendship

I am on vacation, spending a week on a Greek island with my good friend George and some of his other friends and family, which will be followed by a week in Portugal with my wife and children. I have known George for over twenty years now, and yet, the longer I know him, the more I find out about him, and the more I feel connected to the person he is rather than the person I imagine him to be.

We cannot readily distinguish and separate friendship from love. When we make friends, we typically value certain qualities in those friends; we put aside our egos and accept the others who are our friends as worthwhile, as our equals. Friendship increases our capacity to learn and grow. Through the respect of friendship we can listen to new ideas, accept counsel and support, and overcome challenges (either emotional or practical) that might otherwise defeat us. And, likewise, we do the same for our friends. With friends, we achieve more and live more richly than without friends. Friendship contributes to the persistence of the individual as well as to the persistence of human beings generally. For this reason, we rightly place a high importance on friendship.

As with love, there can be confusion about the term *friendship*. We often say "friend" when we mean "acquaintance." And again, when we consider the underpinnings of true friendship, the quelling of the ego, the acceptance of the value of the other person for who he or she is, we can clearly see the difference. We form acquaintances to achieve a network of useful or valuable contacts or connections. Acquaintanceship is egotistical (often on both sides), whereas we value a true friend for himself or herself, not for anything he or she can do for us. This is not to say that acquaintances have no place in life, or that acquaintanceship is wrong, but when we confuse it with or elevate it to the same status as friendship we lead ourselves astray.

Community

Whether we live in a big city surrounded by millions of strangers or in a remote and tiny village, community will work its way into the fabric of our lives. Even those of us who shun social interactions and local organizations, who forgo the potluck dinners and town hall meetings, who reluctantly nod at our neighbors, inevitably play some role in our community—the minimal social act of taking out the trash involves us in the complex interplay of people living in a connected group. Only the hermit or the recluse can truly claim to live without community, and only then if he or she is self-sufficient.

At many levels and in myriad ways, community contributes to the persistence of our species—community can be protective, supportive, instructive, and collaborative. In a community we share tasks, give assistance and support, pool resources, learn, and grow. Community lets us mitigate risk and combine strength. In a well-functioning community, people act altruistically, accepting that what is good for the group is good for all, understanding that from time to time we need to forgo our own desires for the good of others. A community rallies to the support of its members; the best feelings and ideas come forward and rise to the top. Of course, not all communities function well, and no community is perfect. The chance that all members of a community will act altruistically in all situations is impossibly remote.

An intrinsic risk of community is that the community develops a group ego that becomes self-serving and directed against outsiders or other communities, or that tends to ostracize those members of the community who don't conform. In almost all communities, some element of group ego exists and works against the overall benefit of the community or of people in general.

Communities of any size tend to contain smaller communities and groups. At the broadest level, all living organisms are members of the community of life. On a more pragmatic basis, all human beings belong to the community of human life on earth, within which we have communities that form along geographical, religious, political, racial, and social lines. The smallest community contains two persons involved in a relationship.

As individuals, we can add greatest value to persistence by remaining alert to the benefits and dangers of community. As with love, we cannot simply accept the will of the group if we feel that it derives from a narrow and inappropriately group-centric perspective. Sometimes our greatest contribution comes from stepping outside the community, setting ourselves in opposition to it.

Work

> "I can't sit still and see another man slaving and working. I want to get up and superintend, and walk round with my hands in my pockets, and tell him what to do."
>
> —Jerome K. Jerome, *Three Men in a Boat*

We can define work as that which we do to serve some purpose beyond the immediate satisfaction of the nonessential desires of the ego. Work can be mopping the floor, it can be earning a livelihood pushing paper in an office, it can be writing a book, it can be caring for an infant, it can be picking apples for a pie. So long as the task involves some end other than the sole satisfaction of the wants of the ego, we can consider it work. Work so defined tends to contribute to the ongoing sustenance of ourselves, our family, society, and humankind.

As an example, reading a book solely for pleasure is not work. Reading a book for school or for research is work. Reading a book to further our understanding, to grow—following our definition—qualifies as work.

Which brings us to the point that not all work is equal. Something we do to further our own understanding or to meet our own needs tends to contribute less to persistence than something we do to help meet the needs of others or society generally. Then again, if we're furthering our own knowledge so that we can make more of a contribution to society at some time in the future, the differentiation becomes less clear. In most cases, there will be overlap and admixture between the different purposes for the task at hand.

As human beings, we seem to be predisposed toward work and toward avoiding work. We can't help ourselves. Despite a desire to do nothing, doing nothing leads to frustration and depression, a sense of unrest. When faced with a daunting task or a great deal of work, we feel overwhelmed and look for ways to procrastinate or reduce the work involved by sharing the load or finding some way to make the work easier. And yet, we feel great satisfaction when we've finished something, the sense of a job well done.

Our capacity for work, and our struggle with the tug and revulsion of work, came about with consciousness. Without consciousness, we have no sense of a choice in what we do, no sense of application or nonapplication, contribution or noncontribution. The nonconscious organism simply does; it does not work. As conscious beings, we retain our nonconscious and immediate instincts, or animal being, and attain a conscious perspective. This dual nature of human existence explains the dual nature of our relationship to work. In order to work, we need to suppress our immediate animal instinct to do only that which we feel compelled to do to ensure our survival or to answer an innate urge. In order to work, we need to conceptualize and value the outcome of the work, or recognize and accept the penalty of nonwork.

Accepting this struggle and finding a balance between these two demands of the self helps us contribute to our persistence and to the persistence of people generally. If we work to the exclusion of all else, we will suffer, and no matter how much we contribute to society generally, society will ultimately tend to suffer, too, because we suffer. If human beings were to evolve into selfless, regimented workaholics, I doubt the human race would survive very long. Because, ultimately, we wouldn't see the point.

For most of us, work means earning a livelihood, keeping a home, raising a family. Those who have experienced idleness between jobs or periods without work know only too well the associated feelings of worthlessness and depression. We want to feel as though we are contributing. On the other hand, when we care more about the prestige or power of our work, when we pay more attention to the trappings of success than to the quality and value of the work we do, we cease to be doing valuable work and have strayed into the satisfaction of the ego. And if we find ourselves doing work that earns a living but from which we derive no sense of worth and value, we are unfortunately missing out on some aspects of the value of work.

Leisure

Today is Saturday. No matter how quickly the week passes (and it seems to pass ever more quickly, the older I get), the weekend passes more quickly. Does this diminish the pleasure of the time away from work or heighten it? Certainly, I'd like the weekends to be longer—three days, four days…at what point does the balance begin to seem wrong?

A hundred years ago, people in America and Europe typically worked six days each week. A hundred years from now, perhaps, the workweek will be four days instead of five. Already some European countries have reduced the number of hours in a workweek and limit the amount of overtime that people can work. The age of mechanization and technological innovation has brought about a situation in which people in the developed world generally don't need to work so hard to achieve the same levels of production and service. And our homes today, our personal lives, require less work, too.

Yet many of us complain about the unrelenting fullness and busyness of our lives—we seem to be filling our time with more things to do, more appointments to keep track of, more places to go, more tasks to take care of. While our lives get easier in some ways, they get more complex and stressful in others.

(When I was growing up in England, my family and I liked to watch a TV show called *The Good Life* in which a typical suburban family renounced the material, modern life and turned their home into a self-sufficient small-holding, with pigs and chickens and homemade everything, much to the horror and bewilderment of their stubbornly materialistic neighbors. The show poked fun at the shallow mores of modern society while asking the deeper question—would we be happier if we had less? The answer it seemed to give was yes. And the show's popularity seemed to indicate that, for many, this answer resonated deeply with a yearning for a simpler life.)

But however we fill the bulk of our time, with long hours at work or meeting the obligations of the modern world, our lives still do include time for leisure. Even those who work long, hard days, with seemingly no time to rest, experience some moments of leisure, however brief and hemmed in by toil.

The concept of leisure differs from that of inactivity. Non-conscious animals don't have leisure time; they simply rest when they have nothing else to do, whereas leisure implies a period of time when our thoughts and bodies can be free from necessary or obligatory activity. Leisure rewards our industry; it is the carrot at the end of the busy stick. An appropriate dose of leisure therefore contributes to persistence by giving a sense of meaning to our labor and by permitting freedom and time for regeneration of thought, energy, and motivation. Once we have had sufficient time to regenerate, we have had sufficient leisure. Too much leisure and we begin to experience feelings of idleness and lack of self-worth and depression.

Creativity

Every conscious act or thought constitutes an act of creation. The consciousness of a single person, of each and every one of us, creates a universe. Consciousness is creativity. As human beings we constantly create concepts. Whether we have created them before or not, and whether or not others have created them before us, each time we bring a concept into awareness, we give birth to that concept.

In a narrower sense, we render creativity as the act of bringing about something new in such a way that others can perceive it, too. In this sense, creativity includes the written and spoken word, painting, sculpture, music. Creativity communicates newness, permits newness—new awareness, new understanding, new ways of responding, new ways of interacting with our surroundings. Without creativity there is no development of understanding, no adaptation through awareness. Creativity contributes to persistence by providing us with the ability to continue to grow, learn, communicate, and adapt.

Many negative connotations associated with creativity again arise through a confusion of concepts. Unoriginal art, inept efforts, pointless or shallow creations give creativity a bad name. If someone paints a worthless picture, one cannot fault art, but only the artist. Attaching unwarranted value to a creative effort also tends to destroy the credibility of creativity as a worthwhile quality. Popularity does not necessarily equal value.

Some dismiss creative pursuits as intrinsically worthless, denying the positive impact of art, while others refuse to discriminate, granting equal and unequivocal importance to any and all creative pursuits. To compound these problems, we share no objective basis for judging the value and creative worth of a particular piece of art. Very often an artist will struggle and toil at his art for a lifetime with little or no recognition, only to be lauded as an innovative genius years after his death. And, of course, the opposite happens, too, when posterity reveals the emptiness of an artist renowned during her lifetime.

As we've explored in the section of this book that deals with understanding universal concepts, beauty has a pure ground in the representation of conceptual objects. One way, then, to assess the value of creativity is to assess the beauty of the result. Another is to assess its contribution to persistence. Using the latter measure, the objective value of a creative work can only be judged at a moment in time and in terms of its contribution to persistence or potential contribution to persistence (past, present, and future) as judged at that moment. (If a song can inspire millions of young people to consider the world with greater selflessness, it will contribute to persistence and holds, objectively, great value. A music critic can point out that the song is derivative or trite, but this doesn't mean that the song is worthless. A song that had little popular value at the time of its writing and did not communicate ideas contributing to persistence, but that later receives acclaim for its lyrical and musical genius and inspires generations of songwriters to come, can be considered, objectively, to hold great value, although of a very different kind, and appearing at a very different time in its life.) We cannot know at the time of creation whether the product of the creative act will ultimately contribute to persistence or not. (This understanding leads us to be kinder to the struggling artist.)

The former approach, then, has more universal meaning: to judge creativity by how well the artist communicates his or her perception and by the perceptiveness being communicated. Communication, whether of a good message or a bad one, accurate or inaccurate, tends to have greater value than no communication. Or, to put it another way, the capacity for communication has developed and evolved because it has tended to improve the persistence of life as a form. Timeless art captures timeless perceptions, pure concepts. The more deeply an artist delves into the underlying truth of his or her perception, the more unchanging and firmly held will be the value of his or her creation.

Life Choices

When I set about writing this book more than two years ago, I had a strong sense of what I wanted to communicate but little idea of how to go about it or what it would mean to commit myself to the work involved. Neither did I realize the possible ramifications of writing such a book and having others read it. Once the initial excitement subsided, I found myself filled with uncertainty, anxiety, and fear. As I set to work, I leaned on the paddle of determination and pushed myself forward over the brink of the first daunting wave and down the other side toward the next, trying not to think about the wide expanse ahead.

Life's choices set us on the ocean of the unknown. We must leave the comforting harbor of the familiar in the hope of reaching an unseen, uncharted, and distant shore of future achievement or failure. We make choices to further our persistence. And we can make choices because we have consciousness. We don't simply react to stimuli, guided by innate impulse; we plan and think and calculate and reflect.

Considerable attention has been given to the possibility that we don't make choices, that our physiological and psychological history determines our acts and actions, that the notion of conscious choice is an illusion, existence's sleight of hand. Of course, practically speaking, it makes no difference. We feel that we have conscious choice and that the world operates as if we do have choice. However, we can perhaps clarify the apparent dichotomy by considering in more detail what we mean by choice, as opposed to selection.

If I am presented with two pieces of paper, one red and one blue, and asked to choose one (not asked which one I prefer, but just asked to make a selection), my choice will seem to be random but conscious. But if I can truly select one or the other, unguided by reason, I am not making a conscious choice; I am acting instinctively. My selection is no more a choice than if I were to randomly take the left or right fork when walking a trail in the woods.

If I am presented with the same situation but my instruction is to choose my favorite color, am I making a conscious choice? Let's presume that preference guides my selection, that I respond to the instruction as directed. My selection then does not involve reason. My amassed experience with and reactions to the respective colors leave me with a general sense of preference for blue or red. I respond consciously to the instruction, but beyond choosing to follow the instruction I am not making a conscious choice— instinct guides my selection or red or blue.

Now if I am told that the piece of paper colored blue represents "cooler" and red "warmer," and that my selection will result in a change in the temperature of the room, I am faced with the possibility of a conscious choice. I can simply select without thinking, but if I wish I can also consider the current temperature and decide whether I want the room to be hotter or cooler. I am faced with a selection that need not be made randomly and will incur consequences. Can my choice be said to be predetermined? My experience with temperatures and my current sense of how warm or cold I am—don't these determine whether I will select blue or red? Yes, but we must not forget that I can choose to take the room temperature in whichever direction I wish. I have not been instructed to make the room more comfortable for myself. I may be cold and choose to make the room cooler. The room may be perfectly comfortable, so that my choice will bring less comfort regardless of whether I make it cooler or hotter. My choice is not constrained. Despite a tendency in one direction or the other, I have the freedom to choose.

But isn't the way in which I respond to such choices predetermined by my psychological makeup? If I perversely choose to make the room cooler when I'm already cold, doesn't my choice reveal a preexisting crookedness in my way of thinking? The answer, of course, can't be anything but yes.

If we take the idea of predetermination to this extreme, however, we're missing the point. Consciousness gives us the ability to make selections through reflection on the concepts at work, to act against instinct, to overcome our nonconscious impulses. When we speak of free will, we speak of the ability to resist and turn away from the instinctive, natural but nonconscious striving of all living things. Free will means simply a will freed of the constraints of the nonconscious. Our conscious will lets us interpret choices conceptually, overcoming the demands of our bodies, our instinctive urges.

So choice, then, means selecting a particular option after bringing the circumstances and consequences of two or more options into our consciousness. And as we've touched on earlier, practically everything we do in life involves choice, even those things that needn't. All of our choices have a purely personal aspect, an aspect that might relate to society generally, and in many cases an aspect that can have an impact on the world around us. Very often these impacts are small. We make thousands of choices each day that are effectively inconsequential in and of themselves. But taken together these choices can make a difference.

Our life choices reflect our personal contribution to and interaction with the universe. Whether it will ultimately end in a slow cold death or a sudden implosion, the universe does exist and we exist as part of it. Our life choices will determine whether we contribute positively to that existence, by positively impacting the persistence of life as a form, or whether our contribution is negative. We each carry the weight of personal choice and the responsibility for playing our part in furthering the persistence of life. At the same time, we each hold within the possibility for an awareness of the lightness at work in existence, the ultimate illusion of the material world, the absence of meaning beyond the meaning of that which presents itself to us.

Appendix: Further Thoughts on the Quantization of Space and Time

We can conceptualize a fundamental particle as a "standing wave"—an energy state confined to a single phase shift in three dimensions. Rather than propagating indefinitely at the speed of light, the energy of a fundamental particle wraps around on itself, thereby creating the familiar dimensions of space. (Although the concept of a standing wave is intended to be illustrative, the model seems to correspond quite closely to the measured energies and inferred dimensions of fundamental particles. And why not? It's unlikely that the nature of particle energy is different from radiation in anything but its constrained state.)

If the masses and energies of fundamental particles take only a discrete range of values, then perhaps these values reflect a fundamental quantization of energy, an indivisible energy fragment. This would also mean that space and time at the very shortest distances and over the very smallest spans must be quantized, too. In other words, the universe consists of discrete, indivisible units of space and time. The smallest unit of space would correspond to the phase dimensions of the fundamental energy quantum. And the smallest unit of time would be consistent with one oscillation (one phase shift) of this energy state. Conversely, if time and space are not quantized, why wouldn't we see a spectrum of fundamental particles?

Time and space are quantized.

On one hand, this conclusion disturbs us. As human beings, we experience space and time as seamless, smooth, essentially indivisible. On the other hand, can we really conceive of the reality of an infinitely divisible distance in space, an infinitely divisible moment of time? Doesn't everything we know about the universe, the quantum nature of the tiniest particles, imply that this seam-lessness is illusory, that on the very smallest scale there must be a unit of energy that can't be subdivided, a distance in space or period in time that we cannot reduce?

Einstein's theory of relativity postulates that the speed of transmission of electromagnetic radiation—the universal constant c—is the same in all frames of reference. If we extend this concept to say that the energy of a material energy state—a fundamental particle—has an effective speed of transmission by virtue of its fre-quency and dimensions, we could postulate that this effective speed of transmission is also constant and equal to c. The fre-quency of the phase shift of a constrained energy state (a funda-mental particle) multiplied by the effective diameter of the particle (the equivalent wavelength) also equals c. We can therefore express the quantization of fundamental energy states (and also space and time) through the following functions.

If E is the energy (mass) of a fundamental particle (a lepton or a quark), then

- the corresponding frequency f of this energy state equals E divided by Planck's constant h (that is, $f = E/h$),
- the corresponding fundamental quantum of time T equals 1 divided by f (that is, $T = 1/f$),
- and the corresponding fundamental quantum of space W equals the universal constant c divided by E and then multiplied by h (that is, $W = h \times c/E$).

It follows that the most massive fundamental particle will define the smallest quantum of space and time. It also follows that even though electromagnetic radiation appears to cover a continuous spectrum, it cannot do so and must instead respect the fundamen-tal quantization of space and time.

Printed in the United States
72016LV00002B/208-243